THE YEAR IN PICTURES 1973/74

© THE CAXTON PUBLISHING COMPANY LIMITED 1974
A member Company of the British Printing Corporation Limited

Designed and produced by The Caxton Publishing Company Limited, London
Printed and bound in England by Jarrold and Sons Ltd, Norwich

ISBN 0 7014 0026 9

CONTENTS

EDITORIAL LETTER_____ PAGE 4

FOREWORD_____ PAGE 5

DATELIST 1973/74_____ PAGE 6

JULY 1973 TO
JUNE 1974 INCLUSIVE_____ PAGES 8 TO 200

SPORT 1973/74_____ PAGE 201

INDEX_____ PAGE 217

EDITORIAL DIRECTOR_____ DAVID RODRIGUES

EDITOR_____ **PATRICK SCRIVENOR**

ART EDITOR _____ EDWARD J. SIMMONDS

PICTURE EDITOR _____ JUDY LEHANE

SPORTS EDITOR _____ DONALD WOOD

Assistant editor _____ Clare Gunn

Assistant art editors _____ Helen Rix, Catherine Donnellan

Editorial assistant _____ Anne Murray

EDITORIAL LETTER

1973/1974 will be remembered, in Europe anyway, as 'energy crisis' year. Few men-in-the-street had realised how dependent their standard of life was on only one source of energy — oil. As the aftermath of the Arab-Israeli War unfolded — as the Arab oil-producing nations cut down supplies of oil and put up the price — Western Europe, Japan and the US faced a dress rehearsal of what ecologists had been prophesying for nearly a decade; the exhaustion of the earth's available fossil fuels.

To most citizens the foremost short-term effect of the oil shortage was the lack of petrol for motoring, but, for governments and industries, transport was only one area of concern. The shortage of oil to generate electrical power threatened to bring manufacturing industries to a halt, and in Britain, where the situation was compounded by industrial unrest, the government was forced to put the nation on a three-day working week to conserve energy stocks. Other nations adopted other measures: petrol rationing, car-less days, lighting restrictions — in one way or another nearly everyone in the industrialised nations had a tiny foretaste of that elusive date that ecologists called 'doomsday'.

But in many ways the energy crisis was a 'phoney crisis'. The two most important oil-producing states — Saudi Arabia and Iran — were sufficiently anti-Communist never to wish to weaken the West seriously. The total severance of oil supplies, except to Holland and the US, was never threatened. Their real objectives were three: to weaken Western support for Israel; to show consumer nations that they must pay a higher price for their energy supplies; and to make their weight felt before other oil sources and alternative energy technologies weakened their stranglehold. Fewer luxuries and larger energy bills were all that the West had at risk during the crisis.

Not surprisingly in a year of economic crisis, governments came and went with more than usual frequency. In September 1973, the Chilean armed forces ousted President Allende, a move to the right, while in April 1974, the Portuguese armed forces ousted Dr Caetano, a move, if not to the left, at any rate to the centre. At the end of February 1974, the British Conservative government gave way, albeit rather reluctantly, to a Labour government after an indecisive election in which the Liberals and independent groups gained an unprecedented number of seats. Harold Wilson became the leader of Britain's first minority government since the war.

In the US the Watergate crisis forfeited its claim to be called a crisis, if it had not done so already, by entering its third year. The affair was complicated by the saga of the President's tape recordings. Testifying before the senate Watergate Committee, one of the President's aides, Alexander Butterfield, revealed that Nixon recorded all his conversations in his office in the White House. Obviously any such recordings, unbowdlerised, would go a long way to establish the extent of the President's complicity in Watergate. They were accordingly subpoenaed, both by the Committee and by the Special Prosecutor. The President ignored the demand. Pressed again the White House became coy and claimed Executive Privilege. Eventually a short version of the 'relevant' conversations was released, but it was found to have gaps and there was a suspicion that it had been 'edited'. More tapes were demanded. Again the President stalled, and eventually he attempted to by-pass his investigators by making public a transcript of his tapes. Although the book was an instant best-seller, the idea backfired disastrously. The low level of the conversations revealed by the transcript cast serious doubt on Nixon's suitability for his high office, and his popularity, insofar as he had any left, plummeted.

The world's trouble spots — Indo-China, the Middle East, Ulster — remained troubled. In October 1973, the Middle East witnessed the fourth Arab-Israeli War in which, despite early successes, the Egyptian and Syrian forces were decisively beaten. There was little comfort for Israel, however. Her forces were taken by surprise, her losses in *matériel* were huge, and her opponents were disconcertingly resolved and well-armed.

By the end of June 1974, the Western nations had overcome their difficulties with the oil-producing states. The Arab-Israeli dispute was in a state of precarious ceasefire. Watergate had reached a stage where impeachment of the President seemed inevitable. Holland and West Germany were poised to compete for the World Association Football Cup. Chris Evert was on the way to her first Wimbledon Women's Championship, and, apparently, on the way to marriage with Jimmy Connors, her fellow-countryman, who seemed for his own part to be on the way to the Men's Championship.

But all the events of 1973/74 were enacted against a backcloth that had become no less sombre as June 1974 drew to a close — the threat, felt in varying degrees in all countries, of uncontrollable price inflation. Governments struggled to find some way to break the vicious circle of pay and price rises but, by the end of June, none of their efforts had borne fruit.

PATRICK SCRIVENOR

FOREWORD

The saying that a good picture is worth a thousand words has become worn with over-use, but it remains true that a picture triggers off a whole train of associations that a written description would leave undisturbed. Every day we encounter an enormous range of visual information. Headlines in newspapers, advertisements, and television programmes are just a few. The barrage is so intense that most modern citizens are visually 'shell-shocked'. Memories of what has happened are patchy and out of order. The information is absorbed, but not stored.

Do we, however, need to remember all that we see and hear? Perhaps not, but it is a great pity that many people, living in an age when so much information can be come by so easily, have no record of the history they are living through and helping to make.

The Year in Pictures is designed to provide this record. Daily papers and periodical magazines are too bulky and too perishable to provide the same service. Besides, of their very nature they have to publish much that is ephemeral. *The Year in Pictures* brings you the events of twelve months in a packed, concise and, above all, memorable form. The pictures, selected from the world's press and a large number of other sources will provide your own 'news reel' of the year, and the key to unlock all your own memories.

But *The Year in Pictures* is not concerned exclusively with political, economic and military events. They are there, of course, but how many of your memories of the year really centre round major international affairs? Very few probably, and, for this reason, *The Year in Pictures* gives coverage to a wide range of events — major, minor, momentous, trivial — the only common factor between them being that someone was there with a camera.

Since it became possible to reproduce photographs by a printing process, and particularly since the advent of colour reproduction, news photographers have become a numerous and highly skilled band. Strangely, however, outlets for their work are few, and, in bringing their work together between two covers, *The Year in Pictures* hopes to provide a service not only to its readers but to its contributors as well. Each year the editors will select what they consider to be the outstanding news pictures of the year, and photographers will qualify for Caxton Year in Pictures Awards.

The editors feel that as a source of information for you and your family, as an album of memories, and as a pictorial record of your own times, *The Year in Pictures* will provide a valuable yearly addition to your bookshelves.

DAVID RODRIGUES

DATELIST OF THE YEAR: JULY 73/JUNE 74

JULY

1 July: **UK/Ulster**. Unionists poll 39% of the vote in Northern Irish Assembly Elections, gaining 22 of the 78 seats

6 July: **UK/Bahamas**. HRH Prince of Wales attends the Independence ceremonies of the Commonwealth of the Bahamas

8 July: **UK/Sport**. Billie Jean King wins the Wimbledon Women's Singles for the fifth time

8 July: **Italy**. Mariano Rumor becomes Premier of Italy leading a left-centre coalition government

10 July: **UK/Portugal**. *The Times* of London publishers a report alleging the massacre of 400 African villagers in Mozambique by Portuguese troops

10 July: **Italy**. Paul Getty junior is kidnapped in Italy

11 July: **France**. 122 passengers are killed when a Brazilian Boeing 707 crashes near Orly Airport, Paris, France

17 July: **Afghanistan**. King Zahir Shah of Afghanistan is overthrown in a bloodless coup by brother-in-law General Daud Khan

21 July: **France**. France explodes a small nuclear bomb over Mururoa Atoll in the Pacific

28 July: **Khmer Republic**. Rebel forces almost entirely surround the capital, Phnom Penh

28 July: **US/Space**. The Skylab 2 mission blasts off for a space trip of 59 days

AUGUST

3 August: **Canada/Commonwealth**. Queen Elizabeth and delegates from all Commonwealth countries meet in Ottawa for the Commonwealth Conference

7 August: **East Germany**. Eighty-year-old Walter Ulbricht, East German Chancellor, dies

12 August: **UK/France**. The British and French governments sign an agreement for the go-ahead of the Channel Tunnel

15 August: **US/Khmer Republic**. All US bombing missions in support of government forces come to an end

21 August: **Sweden**. Swedish police outwit and capture a bank robber who had been holed up for five days with four hostages in the vault of a Stockholm bank

23 August: **Pakistan**. Floods devastate large areas of Pakistan making thousands homeless

31 August: **Italy**. The death toll reaches 33 in the Naples cholera outbreak

SEPTEMBER

2 September: **Eire**. Two men are rescued from a cable-laying midget submarine trapped 1,500 ft down 95 miles off the coast of Co Cork

5 September: **France**. Three Arab terrorists raid the Saudi Arabian Embassy in Paris

8 September: **Khmer Republic**. The country's third largest city, Kompong Cham is taken by rebels and retaken by government troops causing extensive civilian casualties

9 September: **UK/China**. An exhibition of Chinese archaeological finds opens at London's Royal Academy

10–19 September: **UK**. Nearly 20 people are injured in a spate of IRA bomb attacks in London

11 September: **Chile**. A military coup topples President Allende's regime

12 September: **France/China**. President Pompidou meets Mao Tse-tung during his visit to Peking

18 September: **Jordan**. King Hussein frees all political prisoners, including Palestinian guerrillas

19 September: **Sweden**. Carl Gustaf accedes to the throne at the age of 27

28 September: **Austria**. Arab terrorists secure the closure of the Schoenau Castle transit camp for Soviet Jewish emigrants by kidnapping four Jewish hostages

OCTOBER

4 October: **US/Japan**. More than a thousand Japanese students demonstrate against the continued US naval presence at the Japanese base of Yokosuka

6 October: **Arab-Israeli War**. Egyptian and Syrian forces attack Israeli forces in Sinai and on the Golan Heights

10 October: **US**. Vice-President Spiro T. Agnew resigns 'in the national interest' after allegations of corruption are made against him

10 October: **Arab-Israeli War**. Major tank battles take place as Egyptian forces push into Sinai. Israeli tanks counterattack in the Golan Heights

11 October: **Sweden**. Henry Kissinger and Le Duc Tho win the 1973 Nobel Peace Prize

12 October: **Arab-Israeli War**. Syrian forces are pushed back beyond the 1967 ceasefire line towards Damascus

14 October: **UK**. World motor racing ace Jackie Stewart announces his retirement

15 October: **UK/Iceland**. The Cod War ends as Britain and Iceland sign an agreement limiting Britain's annual catch of cod

17 October: **Arab-Israeli War**. An Israeli task force secures a bridgehead on the West Bank of the Suez Canal

17 October: **US**. Maynard Jackson is elected as the first Negro mayor of a Southern US city – Atlanta, Georgia

17 October: **Australia**. Queen Elizabeth opens the vastly expensive Sydney Opera House

21 October: **US**. Elliot Richardson, the Attorney-General, and William Rucklehaus resign as Nixon refuses to surrender the White House tapes and dismisses Archibald Cox, the Watergate Special Prosecutor

22 October: **Music**. Pablo Casals, the world's greatest cellist, dies aged 96

23 October: **Arab-Israeli War**. Israeli Commandos capture Mount Hermon

24 October: **Arab-Israeli War**. Final UN ceasefire takes effect. Talks to bring about a disengagement begin at Kilometre 101. UN peacekeeping troops arrive

31 October: **Eire**. Three Provisional IRA leaders are sprung from Mountjoy jail by the use of a helicopter

NOVEMBER

1 November: **UK**. Father Patrick Fell, 32-year-old Roman Catholic priest, is jailed for 12 years for involvement in an IRA bomb plot

1 November: **Turkey**. Film star Danny Kaye opens the Bosphorus Bridge

14 November: **UK**. Princess Anne marries Captain Mark Phillips in Westminster Abbey

14 November: **UK**. The Price sisters receive life imprisonment for their part in the 1973 London car bombings

16 November: **US/Space**. The Skylab 3 space mission blasts off

16 November: **Arab-Israeli War**. Israeli and Egypt sign a ceasefire and disengagement agreement at Kilometre 101

17 November: **UK**. Gerald Nabarro, the flamboyant Conservative MP, dies aged 60

19 November: **Greece**. Tanks and demonstrators meet in the streets of Athens as students of the Athens polytechnic gather to demand an end to the Papadopoulos regime

25 November: **Greece**. A military coup led by Lieutenant-General Ghizikis brings down the Papadopoulos regime

27 November: **US**. Rose Mary Woods, Nixon's private secretary, claims that she might accidentally have erased 18 minutes of conversation between John Dean and the President from one of the White House tapes

DECEMBER

1 December: **Israel**. David Ben Gurion, founder of the State of Israel, dies aged 87

3 December: **USSR/UK**. Sir Alec Douglas Home arrives in Moscow for talks on Anglo-Soviet relations

3 December: **US/Space**. The US spacecraft *Pioneer 10* arrives at its closest point to the planet Jupiter sending back extensive and valuable information

9 December: **UK/Ireland**. All interested parties, except representatives of Ulster's Protestant majority, reach agreement in the Sunningdale talks about the future of Ireland

15 December: **Italy**. Paul Getty junior is released by his kidnappers for a ransom rumoured to be almost £1m

17 December : Italy. Arab terrorists kill 40 people as they fire on waiting passenger queues and toss bombs into a crowded plane at Rome Airport

20 December : Spain. Admiral Carrero Blanco is killed by a bomb placed under the road in Madrid over which his car passed on his return from Mass

JANUARY
7 January : UK. Soldiers and police mount an alert at London's Heathrow Airport on the eve of the arrival of a new Israeli Ambassador to Britain

7 January : Khmer Republic. In the heaviest fighting for six months insurgent troops take Phnom Penh's Airport, only six miles from the capital itself

7 January : UK/Ulster. Brian Faulkner resigns as leader of the Unionist Party in Northern Ireland but remains Chief Executive of the newly formed Northern Ireland Executive

9 January : Thailand. Student demonstrators protest against the visit of Japanese Prime Minister, Kakuei Tanaka, and against Japanese 'economic imperialism'

15 January : UK. Members of the ASLEF union stage a one-day strike bringing London's rail transport to a standstill

27 January : Cyprus. General George Grivas, EOKA leader and partisan of union with Greece, dies

28 January : Australia. 8,000 are homeless after floods devastate the Brisbane area of Queensland

29 January : UK. H. E. Bates, the prolific writer with over 50 books to his credit, dies aged 68

FEBRUARY
4 February : US. Patricia Hearst, daughter of publishing millionaire Randolph Hearst, is kidnapped from her home in Berkeley, California, by the self-styled Symbionese Liberation Army

7 February : Grenada. Amid popular unrest against the island's leader, Eric Gairy, Grenada becomes independent

8 February : UK. Britain's mine-workers strike in support of a wage claim exceeding the government's Phase 3 wage inflation policy

14 February : West Germany. Alexander Solzhenitsyn holds a press conference following his expulsion from the USSR

20 February : Israel. Golda Meir forms Israel's first minority government, a coalition holding only 58 seats of the 120-seat Knesset

21 February : Arab-Israeli War. The last Israeli troops evacuate the West Bank bridgehead on the Suez Canal seized in October

28 February : UK. Britain's electorate goes to the polls in a General Election called by Edward Heath to resolve the economic crisis caused by the fuel shortage and the miner's strike

MARCH
3 March : France. 345 people die in the world's worst air crash to date as a Turkish DC10 explodes and crashes into the ground a few minutes after take-off from Orly Airport

5 March : UK. Harold Wilson returns to 10 Downing Street to head a minority Labour government after an inconclusive General Election result

7 March : US. John Erlichman, the Nixon White House aide who resigned over Watergate, is indicted again on charges connected with the Ellsberg case

19/20 March : UK. Princess Anne escapes uninjured from an attempt to kidnap her

28 March : France. Alain Colas sails his trimaran *Manureva* into St Malo harbour after a record world circumnavigation of 168 days

APRIL
1 April : Iraq. Kurdish tribesmen rout an Iraqi brigade

2 April : France. Georges Pompidou, President of the Republic for five years, dies aged 62

3 April : US. The Congressional Committee on Internal Revenue recommends that President Nixon pay $476,431 outstanding income tax

3/4 April : US. 336 people are killed as the worst onslaught of tornados for 49 years devastates 11 midwestern states

10 April : Israel. Mrs Golda Meir, Israel's Prime Minister resigns

13 April : UK. The body of Kenneth Lennon, the man who claimed to have been recruited by the British Special Branch to infiltrate the IRA, is found in a ditch in Surrey

21 April : UK. Ronald Milhench, the man at the centre of the land scandal involving the forged use of the Prime Minister's signature, is charged with criminal deception

25 April : Portugal. A military coup led by General Spinola topples the Caetano regime

28 April : Israel/Syria. Fighting flares up along the whole Golan Front as the Syrians try to recapture Mount Hermon

MAY
1 May : US. The transcripts of the White House tapes released by President Nixon are put on sale by the government printing office

6 May : West Germany. Willy Brandt resigns from the West German Chancellorship as a result of revelations of spying by a member of his entourage

12 May : UK/Ulster. Northern Ireland's overwhelmingly Protestant working class calls a province-wide strike

14 May : UK. Dr Coggan, the Archbishop of York, is appointed Archbishop of Canterbury in succession to Dr Ramsey

15 May : Israel. Nineteen people die as three Arab terrorists raid an Israeli school and hold hostage the children inside

16 May : Portugal. General Spinola becomes the twelfth President of the Portuguese republic

17 May : Eire. Twenty-seven people are killed as three car bombs explode in Dublin

18 May : India. The Indian government announces the test of an atomic bomb, while adding assurances that all India's atomic development will be for peaceful purposes

24 May : UK. Marcia Williams, Harold Wilson's private secretary, is elevated to a life peerage

27 May : France. Valery Giscard d'Estaing wins the French Presidential Elections with a narrow lead from his nearest rival François Mitterand

28 May : UK/Ulster. Brian Faulkner, head of the Northern Ireland Executive, resigns as the two-week strike by Protestant workers brings the province to total economic standstill

31 May : Syria/Italy. An agreement for a disengagement in the Golan Heights is reached between Syria and Israel

JUNE
1 June : UK. At the Nypro factory at Flixborough in the north of England 29 people are killed as an accidental explosion rips through the chemical works

7 June : UK/Ulster. The Price sisters, jailed for their role in the 1973 Westminster car bombings, abandon their hunger strike after agreement is reached about their eventual transfer to Northern Ireland

7 June : Zambia. Portuguese and Frelimo representatives meet in Lusaka to discuss the future of Mozambique

8 June : UK. A military-style procession accompanies the coffin of Michael Gaughan, the dead IRA hunger striker, through London

10 June : UK. The Duke of Gloucester, only remaining brother of George VI, dies aged 74

12 June : US/Middle East. President Nixon arrives in Egypt on the first stage of his whirlwind tour of the Middle East

13 June : West Germany. The World Cup football series opens in Munich

14 June : Austria. The Russian ballet dancers, Valery and Galina Panov, arrive in Vienna after the successful outcome of their two-year struggle to emigrate from the USSR to Israel

15 June : UK. Two die after clashes between police and left-wing demonstrators in London's Red Lion Square

17 June : UK. A bomb planted by the IRA explodes in a canteen in the Houses of Parliament complex, starting serious fires and threatening the 14th-Century Westminster Hall

25 June : Eire. Dr Rose Dugdale, self-styled freedom fighter for Ireland, is jailed for nine years for her part in the theft of paintings worth over £6m from the home of Sir Alfred Beit

27 June : France/Iran. The state visit of the Shah of Iran to France culminates in an agreement guaranteeing France's oil supplies in exchange for French help in establishing nuclear power plants in Iran

JULY

11 July: **The scene near Orly** Airport, Paris, after a Brazilian Boeing 707 had crashed. Air traffic control at Orly heard the pilot mention engine trouble and a fire on board. Seconds later the aircraft crashed into a nearby field, killing the crew and 122 passengers

Below **1 July: Mr Brian Faulkner,** leader of the Ulster Unionist Party, looks on contentedly with his son and daughter as voting slips are piled into his slot at the Downpatrick counting centre. The Unionists polled 39·3% of the vote and won 22 of the 78 Assembly seats which were distributed among the 12 Northern Ireland Westminster constituencies. Mr Faulkner was elected on the first count at Down South with 16,287 first preference votes in these, the first elections for the new Ulster Assembly

Right **8 July: Signor Mariano Rumor,** 58, pictured here after his appointment as Premier of Italy at the head of a coalition of Christian Democrats, Socialists, Social Democrats and Republicans. Signor Rumor's policy stressed the importance of halting the rise in inflation without affecting adversely the rate of economic growth. He wanted a reorganisation of the system of public finance and a reformation of the tax system. Other items on the agenda were reforms in the penal code, prison regulations and the structure of the judicial system

Agenzia Giornalistica Italia

Press Association

Associated Press

Left **20 July:** **Elizabeth Taylor,** flamboyant actress and film star, is met by her fifth husband Richard Burton, the Welsh actor and Shakespearian lecturer, at Rome's Ciampino Airport after their much-publicised, three-week trial separation. The Burtons' stormy marriage had already survived nine years of arguments and reconciliations and a life spent jet-setting around the world in between bouts of filming

Below **10 July:** **Paul Getty III,** grandson of the US oil millionaire, (*on right*) shares an uncomfortable perch with a couple of friends shortly before his kidnapping in Rome. At first his disappearance was thought to be a hoax, but a ransom demand of $1 m, coupled with threats to his life, convinced the Italian police that the kidnapping was genuine. His millionaire grandfather refused at first to hand over any ransom money out of consideration for the safety of his other grandchildren

Rex Features

Associated Press

16 July 1973: Watergate. Enter the 'Tapes'. June ended on a note of climax in the Watergate affair. After the allegation of Mr John Dean, made before the Senate Watergate Committee, that President Nixon was involved in the 'cover-up', it seemed that July could have little to offer. The expected rebuttals of Mr Dean came from more loyal White House aides, notably Mr Mitchell the former US Attorney-General, but the bombshell of the month was dropped, almost casually, by Nixon's archive chief, Mr Butterfield, who revealed that the President recorded all his conversations on tape. Obviously any such tapes could settle at once the extent of the President's involvement in Watergate and other related scandals and, on the 23rd, both the Senate Committee and Archibald Cox, the Watergate special prosecutor, issued subpoenas binding the President to produce a number of recordings and documents in court by 26 July. The President's reaction was to ignore the subpoenas, and the constitutional deadlock continued until the end of the month

Left **The fish-eye lens** captures the tense atmosphere of the Senate Committee in session

Above **25 July: Senators Ervin** and Baker raise their hands in the Committee's unanimous vote to subpoena the President to make available his tape-recordings

Below **1 July: Ronnie Peterson,** the Swedish racing driver, wins the French Grand Prix in his Formula 1 John Player Special Lotus

London Art Tech.

13

Sygma

Right **21 July: France explodes** a small nuclear bomb over Mururoa Atoll in the Pacific. The explosion, which the French refused to confirm or deny, was believed to be a triggering device for a larger bomb. The incident followed weeks of build-up in which protests had become so widespread and bitter that a more sensitive administration would have called off the tests. French apologists for the tests appeared not to grasp the now established fact of cumulative radio-activity in the atmosphere. The strongest protests came from nations in and around the Pacific, and New Zealand sent a frigate, the *Otago*, to defy the zone prohibited to shipping by the French

Below **The 'Otago'** steams into troubled waters

Sygma

Associated Press

Above **29 July: President Papadopulous** of Greece casts his vote in the referendum that gave a 90% 'Yes' to the regime's constitutional proposals for the establishment of a republic. The turn-out was large, but many of the regime's opponents complained of improper electoral procedures, including failure at some polls to distribute the 'No' as well as the 'Yes' papers

Syndication International

Below **17 July: King Zahir Shah** of Afghanistan is overthrown in a bloodless coup by his brother-in-law and former Prime Minister, General Daud Khan. Total resistance to change had characterised Shah's rule, and the coup was quickly consolidated and recognised by the outside world. China, however, remained cool to the new regime, suspecting Russian influence

Below **18 July: Afghan soldiers** on the alert in the Khyber Pass immediately after the coup

Stern

Associated Press

Camera Press/Sophie Baker

Above **18 July: Jack Hawkins, CBE,** the much-loved actor, dies aged 62 after an operation on his larynx. Hawkins underwent an operation to remove a cancerous growth from his throat in 1966 and although he learnt to speak by using his stomach muscles and diaphragm he was never satisfied with his new way of speech. In April 1973 he went to New York for a dangerous operation to fit an artificial voice-box. The operation was unsuccessful and he developed an infection. He suffered recurrent haemorrhages and died as a result of secondary bleeding of an artery

Associated Press

Above **6 July: Diana Rigg marries.** The 33-year-old fiercely independent actress sacrificed her independence to marry her 'perfect partner'. He is Israeli artist Manachen Gueffen. It was his second marriage. The couple sneaked off to the Chelsea Register Office, London, and managed to avoid all publicity until after the event

Above **6 July: HRH the Prince of Wales,** who was representing the Queen, is met by Bahamian Prime Minister Lynden O. Pindling and his wife as he arrives at Nassau for the Independence celebrations. The official Commonwealth of the Bahamas became an independent nation within the Commonwealth at midnight on 9 July

24 July: Libyan officials look on as smoke pours from a Jumbo jet on Benghazi airfield. This was the culmination of one of the most involved hijacking sagas of the early 1970s. On 19 July the Boeing 747, belonging to Japan Air Lines, was hijacked over the Netherlands and diverted to Dubai on the Persian Gulf. The hijackers, three Arabs and one Japanese, demanded the release of Kozo Okamoto, jailed for his role in the Lydda massacre of 1972. The Dubai authorities refused to negotiate with the hijackers and the plane remained on the sweltering tarmac of Dubai's airfield for three days, surrounded by police and troops. Later the hijackers were allowed to refuel and take off. Hoping for more sympathetic treatment they landed in Libya but, finding the Libyan attitude equally intransigent, they released the hostage passengers and destroyed the aircraft

Below **22 July: The Jumbo jet,** and its 143 passengers, waits on Dubai airfield for the hijackers' next move

Below **24 July: The last moments** before the Boeing completely disintegrated

Associated Press

Rex Features

Left **29 July: The destruction** of the Larnaca Road police station in Nicosia by members of the EOKA underground was part of a series of clashes between armed supporters of General Grivas and the Cyprus government's security forces which intensified in July 1973. The Minister of Justice, Mr Christos Vakis, was kidnapped from his Nicosian home by two armed men in military uniform. Mr Vakis was released just over a month later. Twenty-one arrests were made of prominent pro-Grivas Greek Cypriots

Right **3 July: Betty Grable,** whose legs were insured for a million dollars, dies of lung cancer aged 65. Miss Grable, who was reputed to be the highest-paid woman in the US between 1946 and 1947, worked right up until the year before her death when her illness made it impossible for her to carry on. In her lifetime she earned $3m net from her films, which grossed $100m, and 'pin-up' pictures of her were bought by more than 3m troops in the Second World War

Below **July 1973: Paddy McMahon** on Penwood Forgemill wins the Men's European Show Jumping Championship at Hickstead, England

Associated Press

Colorsport

19

July 1973: The war in Indo-China. During July 1973 the forces of President Lon Nol of the Khmer Republic fought under the threat, announced on 29 June, of an end to US bombing support on 15 August. In the meantime US air strikes rose to a daily average of 200, but to little avail. Government troops were constantly forced back by the Sihanoukists until, by the end of the month, the capital Phnom Penh was surrounded by up to 30,000 rebels within eight miles of the city at their nearest approach. In South Vietnam the task of supervising the 'ceasefire' continued. Although breaches of the ceasefire remained at a lower level than in April and May, widespread fighting continued

Right **As rebel forces close in** on Phnom Penh government troops administer first aid in the field

Below **August, 1973. Khmer Republic** troops receive a hand-out of US rations. Although bombing support stopped, US logistic support continued

Below right **Despite excellent US equipment** like these armoured personnel carriers, government forces of the Khmer Republic were consistently outclassed by the Sihanoukist rebels during 1973

Donald McCullin/Sunday Times

Rex Features

Rex Features

Colorsport

Don Morley, Sportsworld

Sven Simon

Left **14 July: Effort and concentration** on the face of Cornelia Ender of East Germany as she sets the women's world record for the 100 metres butterfly stroke in 1 minute 2·31 seconds. She had previously set the record for this event at 1 minute 3·05 seconds in April

Above left **8 July: Billie-Jean King** (US) stretches to return a low ball in her final match against Chris Evert (US) in the Wimbledon Women's Singles. Mrs King won the match 6–0, 7–5 to become champion for the fifth time

Above right **Jan Kodes of Czechoslovakia,** robbed of much of the top male competition by the decision to boycott Wimbledon by 73 members of the Association of Tennis Professionals, wins in three straight sets against Alexander Metreveli, 6–1, 9–8, 6–3

Gamma/Mac George

Associated Press

Above **10 July: The site of a massacre?** On 10 July a report was published in *The Times* by Father Adrian Hastings, a British Roman Catholic priest, alleging atrocities in Mozambique. Father Hastings included in his report a detailed account of an alleged massacre in a village called Wiriyamu where over 400 people were thought to have been either shot, burnt or battered to death. The Portuguese government issued a statement repudiating the allegations and claiming that the report was an attempt to cause trouble on the eve of Dr Caetano's official visit to Britain. British journalists subsequently went out to Mozambique to discover the facts behind the alleged atrocities but found no solid evidence of any large-scale massacres

Right **The two Spanish missionaries** with the Burgos Fathers, Father Miguel Buendia, 29 (*left*), and Father Enrique Ferando, 38 (*right*), who handed over the documented evidence of the alleged Wiriyamu massacre to Father Hastings

Sygma/Genevieve Chauvel

Left **21 July: A demonstration** made up by some members of the 40,000 'marchers to Egypt' try to convince their leader Colonel Gaddafi to remain head of the Libyan Revolutionary Command Council. The 40,000 Libyans intended to march to Cairo in the hope of pressing President Sadat of Egypt into agreeing to a total union of the two countries by the appointed date of 1 September 1973. The marchers, on reaching the border, which had been evacuated by Egyptian customs officials to symbolise the end of 'barriers to unity', bulldozed the wooden customs' sheds and marched on to Mersa Matruh. There they ignored the deputation, and the tents erected to house them during discussions, and went on to Fouka, only 200 miles from Cairo, before they were halted. A 21-man delegation was invited to proceed to Cairo where the 'unity petition' signed with 'the blood of Libyan women' was presented to President Sadat. He expressed support for the union but said that 'enthusiasm and emotional impulses' were not 'a sufficient basis for unity'

Below **23 July: A petition in blood.** President Anwar Sadat receives the 'historical document' written 'with the blood of Libyan women' from members of the 21-man delegation pressing for a Libyan/Egyptian merger by 1 September 1973

Associated Press

Associated Press

Associated Press

28 July: Skylab 2 blasts off.
1973 was the year of Skylab, with three missions, each one longer than the last. On 22 June the Skylab 1 crew splashed down after a record 28 days in space, and on 28 July the crew of Skylab 2 took off on what was to be a total of 59 days. Nor were these missions hitchless technical walkovers. The crew of Skylab 1 had to contend with the loss of the vital solar screens, and the Skylab 2 venturers were overcome by acute and debilitating space sickness during the first days of the mission

Skylab 1 in orbit. The brown area is the improvised parasol solar shield protecting the orbital workshop

Left **28 July: Garriott, Lousma and Bean**, the Skylab 2 team, *en route* to the launching pad and (*left*) on their way up

24

AUGUST

John Hillelson

Left **20 August: Nixon rounds** on his Press Secretary, Ron Ziegler: 'I don't want any Press around me. You take care of them.' The incident happened in New Orleans where the President was attending a meeting of US war veterans. The visit had already been overcast by rumours of an attempt to assassinate the President

Below **15 August: President Nixon** meets the Press after his TV broadcast to the nation in which he accepted responsibility for Watergate, 'because it occurred under my administration', but insisted that he 'knew nothing and did nothing'

Associated Press

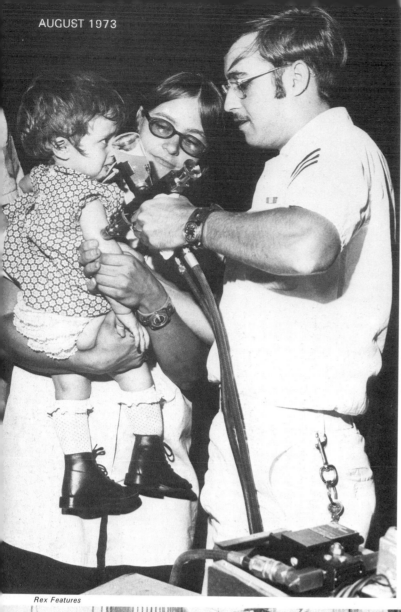

Rex Features

Left **31 August: A frightened little girl** is just one of the thousands who received the intimidating-looking cholera inoculation

Below **31 August: A sanitation truck** sprays disinfectant through the streets of Naples in an effort to check the outbreak of cholera. Thirty-three people died there and naval divers were brought in to destroy the mussel beds in the Gulf of Naples, thought to be the only source of contamination. Queues of people thousands long waited patiently for their inoculations. Tourism plummeted by 80%; the sale of shellfish was banned and all the beaches round the bay were cordoned off. It was the worst cholera outbreak in Italy for over 50 years

Rex Features

Gamma/Jean Claude Francolon

Associated Press

Above **7 August: Herr Willy Stoph,** to become the new East German Head of State, and Erich Honecker, First Secretary of the Socialist Unity Party, attend the funeral of former Head of State, Herr Walter Ulbricht, who died aged 80. He was one of the founders of the German Communist Party and the creator of the Berlin Wall. He was regarded as the last Stalinist leader in Eastern Europe

Right **14 August: French riot police** keep the workers of the Lip watch factory at bay. The Lip factory, France's largest watch factory, was taken over by the workers when the plant became bankrupt. Over 3,000 police stormed the factory at dawn and managed to expel the workers with the minimum of violence on either side

27

Below **12 August: British troops
halt** the People's Democracy
march organised to demand the
release of interned IRA suspects. The
marchers had intended to march to
Long Kesh, site of Ulster's largest
internment camp

12 August: The destination of
the protest march, Long Kesh camp.
The hessian screens were made
necessary by the crazy Northern
Irish situation in which it was
perfectly possible that loyalist
extremists might fire into the camp
to kill suspected Republicans

Pacemaker Press

Associated Press

Sygma/Osborn

Press Association

Above **11 August: Crowds look on** 'as police dig up yet another grave in a horrifying sex murder case where over 20 bodies of young boys, horribly mutilated, were unearthed. Dean Corll, who was responsible for the killings, was murdered himself by one of his homosexual followers, Wayne Henley

Left **6 August: Oil threat to Pembrokeshire.** The Liberian tanker, *Dona Marika*, is seen aground on the rocks of Lindsway Bay with 5,000 tons of oil aboard

Associated Press

Above **8 August: Vice-President Spiro T. Agnew** denounces the charges of corruption made against him as 'false, scurrilous and malicious' and claimed that he had nothing to hide. The charges related to alleged bribery during his governorship of Maryland

5 August: The scene at Athens Airport after Arab terrorists had opened fire, killing three and wounding 55 people

Magnum/J. P. Paireault

AUGUST 1973

Right **15 August: The last B-52** bomber to bomb the Khmer Republic returns to its Thailand base. On 15 August the congressional approval of the bombing ended, and the last mission was flown. US aircraft continued, however, to fly logistic and mercy missions

Below **August 1973: Government troops** in Khmer hit back at encircling rebel forces in an attempt to relieve Highway 4, one of Phnom Penh's main arteries

AFP

Associated Press

August 1973: Rebel troops encamped near Phnom Penh. As fighting engulfed virtually the whole country, worldwide concern was expressed for the safety of Khmer's unique architectural and archaeological remains

Right **3 August**: **The Queen** sits surrounded by Commonwealth leaders at the Ottawa gathering of the Commonwealth Conference. Although British Prime Minister, Edward Heath, outlined a new role for the Commonwealth in a world dominated by the superpowers, the fundamental differences between the 32 attending nations were not raised **Commonwealth leaders** with Her Majesty – *Front row*, 1 Nigeria – General Y. Gowon; 2 Singapore – Lee Kuan Yew; 3 Sri Lanka – Mrs Sirimavo Bandaranaike; 4 Tanzania – Julius Nyerere; 5 The Queen; 6 Canada – Pierre Trudeau; 7 Duke of Edinburgh; 8 Barbados – Errol Barrow; 9 Malta – Dom Mintoff. *Second row*, 10 Cyprus – John Christophides (Foreign Minister); 11 Bangladesh – Mujibur Rahman; 12 India – Swaran Singh (Foreign Minister); 13 Britain – Edward Heath; 14 Mauritius – Sir Ramgoolam; 15 Western Samoa – Fiame Mata'afa; 16 Swaziland – Prince Dlamini; 17 Guyana – S. Ramphal (Minister of Justice); 18 Zambia – Mainza Chona (Vice President); 19 Ghana – Brigadier N. Y. Ashley-Lassen (Chief of Defence Staff); 20 Bahamas – Lynden Pindling. *Third row*, 21 Sierra Leone – Dr Siaka Stevens; 22 Lesotho – Chief Leabua Jonathan; 23 New Zealand – Norman Kirk; 24 Australia – Gough Whitlam; 25 Kenya – Daniel Arap Moi (Vice-President); 26 Jamaica – Michael Manley; 27 Fiji – Ratu Sir Kamisese Mara; 28 Uganda – Paul Etiang (Foreign Minister); 29 Tonga – Prince Tu' Ipelehake; 30 Malaysia – Khir Johari (Minister without Portfolio); 31 Botswana – Sir Seretse Khama; 32 The Gambia – Andrew Camara (Vice-President); 33 Trinidad and Tobago – Francis Prevatt (Minister of Petroleum and Mines); 34 Malawi – J. B. Msonthi (Minister of Education)

Associated Press

Above **7 August**: **Edward Heath** shares a joke with Canada's Premier Trudeau and his wife at an arts gala during the Ottawa Conference

Below **August 1973**: **Off duty in Ulster**. The only comfort, the hard floor of a hangar; the only occupation, weapon-cleaning. A British soldier discovers the true meaning of the maxim that 90% of warfare is boredom

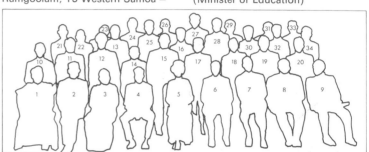

Rex Features

Below **21 August: Love sails into port**. The crew of the 'love raft' *Acali* pose as they reach Cozumel in Mexico. The 11 crew members of the experimental raft travelled from the Canary Isles to the Caribbean, a four-month journey, to see whether people of mixed races and different temperaments could manage to live together in cramped conditions with a total lack of privacy

Sygma/Sylvain Julienne

Above **27 August: Lorries stand idle** during the Chile lorry-driver's strike against President Allende's plans for nationalisation. The drivers, most of them owners of their vehicles, felt threatened by nationalisation, and their strike brought Chile's economy almost to a standstill

Right **29 August: Presidents Gaddafi and Sadat** of Libya and Egypt sign the statement announcing the eventual political merger of their countries

Associated Press

Right **21 August: Bank robber**
Jan Erik Olsson, 31, is led away
handcuffed between two policemen.
Olsson held four people hostage for
five days in the vault of a
Stockholm bank and threatened to
kill them should the police make any
move. Gas was pumped into the
vault through ventilators and the
police rushed in wearing gas
masks and managed to rescue all
four hostages

Embassy of Pakistan

Associated Press

Associated Press

Above right **23 August:
Communications were
shattered** as floods washed over
the railway tracks near Khanpur,
Pakistan. Refugees from the deluge
were forced to wade waist deep in
many places to seek shelter in
temporary camps set up for the
homeless

Right **23 August: The entire
town of Sharaqpur,** only 20
miles from Lahore, was submerged
by the waters flooding the banks of
the River Ravi, making thousands
homeless

37

Below **3 August**: **48 people died**
in this fire as the Summerlands
holiday complex on the Isle of Man
went up in flames. The building,
clad in an acrylic plastic sheeting
widely used in large open structures,
burned terrifyingly fast at a very
high temperature

Press Association

Right **18 August:** **Gordon Banks**, formerly England's World Cup goalie, announced his retirement from football following the loss of the sight in one eye in a car accident. He remained with his old team, Stoke City, in a training capacity

Topix

Above **21 August:** **Mme Funfrock**, fake crown jewels and fake queen. French actress Hugette Funfrock made a series of advertisements for the shop, Samaritaine, which were shown in Paris cinemas in which her accidental resemblance to Queen Elizabeth was used. The advertisements aroused much ill-feeling among British monarchists

Below **14 August:** **Kennedy crashes.** Joseph Kennedy, son of the late Senator Robert Kennedy, overturned his car and injured seven people. One young girl was left partially paralysed. He was charged with negligent driving in a Nantucket court in Massachusetts

Associated Press

Colorsport

Right **21 August: Soviet soldiers** and citizens, spectators at the Moscow Student Games, turn on Jewish supporters of the Israeli basketball team and tear up their Israeli flag

Below right **21 August: Alexander Panaghoulis** walks to freedom after his death sentence for attempted assassination was commuted by the general amnesty for Greek political offenders declared by the Papadopoulos regime on the 21st

Below **21 August: London's noble fire brigade** answer a bomb-scare call to Selfridges. Bombs, planted by the Provisional IRA, had already been found in Liberty's, Marshall and Snelgrove, Harrods and Dickens and Jones

Associated Press   *Popperfoto*

Central Press

SEPTEMBER

12 September: 'Chunnel' work begins as the British and French governments sign the go-ahead for the Channel Tunnel project. Completion date for the Anglo-French rail tunnel was set for 1980 at a cost of £846m

The peripatetic President.
Among his many state visits and travels in 1973 President Pompidou of France became the first Western European head of state to visit China

Left **12 September: As one grand old man** to another: Mao Tse-tung and Pompidou seen together during Pompidou's visit to Peking

Below **11 September: Chou En-lai** toasts the French President on his arrival in China

Bottom **9 September: An exhibition** of Chinese archaeological finds, valued at £20m, opens at the Royal Academy, London. The star of the show was 2,000-year-old Princess Tou, seen here in her magnificent jade burial suit

Gamma/Hugues Vassal

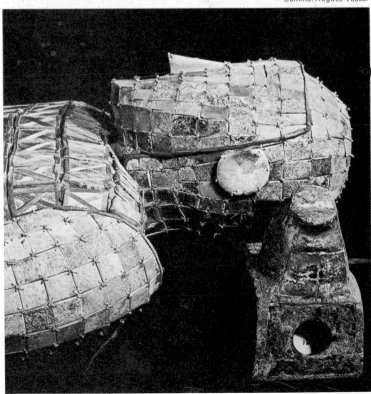

Robert Harding Associates

Associated Press

Above **6 September: David Wilkie of GB** awaiting his award for winning the final of the men's 200 metres breaststroke in Belgrade. Wilkie shattered the world record, in a time of 2 minutes 19·28 seconds, by well over a second in a triumphant victory over former world record holder, John Hencken of the US (*right*)

Right **19 September: The photograph of an Algerian** truck driver, Mohamed Diab, killed at a Versailles police station, is the main feature on one of many such banners carried by anti-racism demonstrators in France. Despite a police ban on the demonstration, several well-known French personalities put in an appearance. Racial prejudice against Algerians in France had been growing and led to the suspension of emigration by Algeria

Rex Features

Associated Press

Sygma/J. P. Laffont

Above **5 September: The head of protocol** at the Saudi Arabian Embassy in Paris is carried off on a stretcher by policemen after leaping from a first-floor window to escape three terrorists from a Palestinian splinter group who were holding 12 other embassy staff hostage

Left **6 September: Less fortunate hostages** are herded, handcuffed onto a Syrian Caravelle, standing by at Le Bourget airport, by one of the terrorists. Their destination was an unnamed Arab capital

September 1973: Mick Jagger, lead singer of the Rolling Stones, leaps back into the limelight at the overwhelmingly successful concert at Wembley's Empire Pool, London. The Stones, who had been quieter than usual in the previous year, rocketed back into the charts with their album *Goat's Head Soup*. This they followed with tours and concerts, using all the new gimmicks, but, in their own inimitable style, their music was more exciting than ever

Laurie Lewis

Popperfoto

Associated Press

Above **18 September: Palestinian political prisoners** celebrate their freedom after King Hussein of Jordan signed an amnesty to release all political prisoners and Palestinian guerrillas

Right **13 September: Lebanese villagers** inspect the remains of a USSR-made MIG 21 shot down by Israeli planes in an engagement with Syrian warplanes. Israel claimed to have destroyed 13 MIGs for only one Mirage lost. Syria admitted to the loss of eight MIGs, but claimed five 'kills' against Israel

Gamma/Charles Gerretsen

Gamma/Charles Gerretsen

Coup d'Etat in Chile, September 1973. On 11 September Chilean army officers staged a successful and violent coup against the government of President Salvador Allende. Allende's attempts to introduce democratic Marxism had led to economic breakdown and catastrophic inflation — justification enough, some would say, for drastic action. But the military leaders tarnished their image, firstly by the excessive bloodiness of their take-over and, secondly, by the large-scale purge of supposed opponents that took place after the coup

Above 11 September: **Troops** in Santiago take cover from the sniping of Allende supporters

Left 11 September: **The Presidential Palace burns** after being bombed by jet aircraft. In it the body of Allende was later found, having apparently committed suicide

Right 11 September: **Civilians** found in the Presidential Palace are searched by soldiers

Gamma/Charles Gerretsen

49

21 September: Bobby Riggs, sport's most publicised male-chauvinist, leaps the net to congratulate Billie Jean King, five times Wimbledon champion, after she had beaten him in three straight sets. The winner stood to get $100,000 and, officially, the loser received nothing. But Riggs was left laughing with an estimated $80,000 in his pocket which he made from the publicity of the world-wide coverage of this battle of the sexes

Popperfoto

Popperfoto

September 1973: Khmer fights on. After the suspension of the US bombing in August, the fighting in the Khmer republic entered a new and, for the government, desperate phase. Sihanoukist and Communist forces fought into the outskirts of Phnom Penh, and Khmer's third largest city, Kompong Cham, was the scene of bitter fighting as the rebels tried to take it

Left **22 September: A republican soldier** grimaces at the detonation of his 105mm mortar

Below **September 1973: Wounded** await evacuation near Phnom Penh

Bottom **8 September: Soldiers stand guard** over the bodies of civilians killed in the fighting in Kompong Cham

Rex Features

Gamma/John Giannini

Far left **19 September**: **The funeral procession** of Tommy Herron, former UDA leader, wends its way to Belfast cemetery. Herron, reported missing from his home, was found murdered on the 17th

Left **17 September**: **British troops** survey the scene of wreckage in King Street, Belfast, after a car bomb had exploded. No one was injured

September 1973: **A spate of bomb** explosions, the work of the Provisional IRA, caused damage and injury throughout London

Below **19 September**: **Damage at** the transport park of the Duke of York's Barracks. Five people were injured

Bottom **10 September**: **The snack bar at Euston Station,** London, after a bomb had exploded. In this attack, and a similar one at King's Cross, 13 people were injured

Pacemaker Press

Associated Press

Popperfoto

Left **September 1973: The last trainload** of Soviet Jews arrives in Vienna before the closing of the Schoenau transit camp

Right **28 September: Heavily armed** Austrian policemen bargain with two Arab terrorists. The terrorists had kidnapped four Jewish hostages from a train *en route* to the Schoenau Castle transit camp for Soviet Jews. The Austrian Chancellor closed the camp in response to the terrorists' demands

Popperfoto

Right **25 September: Frogmen hook up** the recovery lines to the *Skylab 2* command module after splashdown. The three astronauts Jack Lousma, Owen Garriott and Alan Bean waited until the module was safely on board the USS *New Orleans* before extracting themselves from the close confines of the spacecraft which had been their home for a record 59 days in space

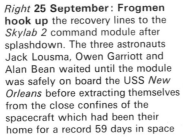

Magnum/M. Faust

Associated Press

Right **19 September: Carl XVI Gustaf of Sweden** accedes to the throne after the death of his grandfather, King Gustaf VI Adolf, aged 90, four days previously. Much younger than his grandfather, who was 68 when he became king, Carl XVI Gustaf was only 27. The position of the Swedish monarchy had been revised in a new constitution to take effect in 1975, but the old king was expressly excluded from the new provisions. Not so his grandson, whose power was to be considerably restricted

Associated Press

Associated Press

Above **2 September: The trapped men,** Roger Malinson (*left*) and Roger Chapman, grin their relief at being rescued from the midget submarine, *Pisces III*. The *Pisces*, engaged in a cable-laying operation, was trapped 1,500ft below sea level, 95 miles off the coast of Co Cork, Eire, for 76 hours before it was brought safely to the surface

Right **2 September: The 19ft long 'Pisces III'** midget submarine in which the two men were incarcerated for over three days

Associated Press

October 10, 1973

Dear Mr. President:

As you are aware, the accusations against me cannot be resolved without a long, divisive and debilitating *struggle in the Congress* and in the Courts. I have concluded that, painful as it is to me and to my family, it is in the best interests of the Nation that I relinquish the Vice Presidency.

Accordingly, I have today resigned the Office of Vice President of the United States. A copy of the *instrument of resignation is enclosed.*

It has been a privilege *to serve with you. May I express* to the American people, through you, my deep gratitude for their confidence in *twice* electing me to be Vice President.

Sincerely,

/s/ Spiro T. Agnew

The President
The White House
Washington, D.C.

OCTOBER

Popperfoto

Rex Features

Above **10 October: Spiro T. Agnew** pictured after the announcement of his resignation on the grounds of national interest. His letter of resignation (*top*) was the result of charges of corruption against Agnew during his term as Governor of Maryland

Left **12 October: Gerald Ford,** seen here with his wife, is nominated US Vice-President in succession to Spiro Agnew

Right **14 October**: **Students** crouch behind a bus to dodge police bullets during a riot in Bangkok. The riots grew out of a peaceful demonstration of 200,000 Thais, most of them students. Police opened fire killing more than 50 students and wounding hundreds. The demonstrators demanded the resignation of Field-Marshal Thanom Kittikachorn and his military government. Kittikachorn's resignation was accepted by the King and the Field-Marshal left immediately for Japan. The Rector of Thammassat University, Professor Sanya Dharmasaki, was invited to form a new Government which included only three soldiers

Below **4 October**: **The US aircraft carrier,** *Midway*, docks at number six pier at the US naval base at Yokosuka. Over a thousand left-wing students marched in protest against the use of Yokosuka as *Midway*'s home port

Associated Press

Associated Press

14 October: Three times world Champion racing driver Jackie Stewart announces his retirement. Stewart, one of racing's most popular figures and a brilliant but careful driver, made the announcement at a celebration party in London to mark his victory in the Belgian Formula I Grand Prix

Popperfoto

Popperfoto

Left **17 October: The Sydney Opera House.** On the 17th Queen Elizabeth and Prince Philip arrived to open the huge, costly, beautiful opera house standing on a promontory in Sydney's famous harbour. More a complete arts centre than just an opera house, the project eventually cost more than ten times its budgeted price

Above **19 October: The Queen signs** the document changing her title to Queen of Australia. Gough Whitlam (*right*) looks on

Below **11 October: As one Nobel prizewinner** to another. Kissinger and Le Duc Tho seen at the successful Vietnam ceasefire talks for which they gained the 1973 Nobel Peace Prize on the 11th

Rex Features

Magnum/Bruno Barbey

Below **21 October**: **Elliot Richardson** (*top*), the US Attorney-General, pictured after his resignation in protest against Nixon's refusal to allow further court action on the Watergate tapes. William Rucklehaus (*bottom*) resigned as Deputy Attorney-General a day later following Nixon's dismissal of Archibald Cox, the Watergate special prosecutor

Associated Press

Associated Press

Above right **29 October**: **Archibald Cox** after his dismissal by Nixon as the Watergate prosecutor. Sacked on a technicality, Cox was getting close in his investigations to embarrassing details of Nixon's own financial dealings and tax situation

Right **26 October**: **Demonstrators** outside the White House demand the President's impeachment

Gamma/Leroy Woods

Magnum/R. Freeman

Press Association

Left **16 October: The stormy** petrel of English football, Brian Clough, leaves Derby County with Peter Taylor after six years as Manager and Assistant Manager. Given to outspoken criticism of both colleagues and superiors, Clough's relations with the Derby County Board had been strained for some time

Below **17 October: Despondent** England players (*left to right*) Tony Currie, Paul Madeley, Martin Peters (Captain), Mike Channon and Roy McFarland trudge off Wembley's soccer pitch after being knocked out of the World Cup. The England side fought well in the second leg of their match against Poland but failed to get past the brilliant Polish goalkeeper, Tomaszewski, more than once. The result was a draw at 1–1, but England needed a victory to qualify

Press Association

Rex Features

Magnum/P. Jones Griffiths

October 1973: The fourth Arab-Israeli war. On 6 October Syrian and Egyptian forces launched simultaneous offensives against the Israeli forces stationed in the areas conquered in the Six-Day War, Sinai and the Golan Heights. The attacks were timed to coincide with the Jewish religious holiday, Yom Kippur. By the time the UN-negotiated ceasefire took effect on the 24th, Saudi Arabia, Jordan, Morocco and Iraq had all sent forces to fight with the Syrians, and the fortunes of war had carried the Israelis from near defeat to a supreme commanding position. Israeli casualties amounted to 1,800 dead and about the same number wounded — enormous losses against the smallness of her regular forces. No reliable figures are available for Arab losses.

A feature of the war was the toll taken of Israeli aircraft by USSR-

Gamma/Michel Laurent

Rex Features

made SAM missiles, and the superiority of the British and American-made Israeli tanks over the Arab's Soviet 'T' type tanks.

Left **October: Sinai.** The wreckage of a gun emplacement after a direct hit

Top left **October: Suez Canal, West Bank.** USSR-made SAM-3 missiles, mainly responsible for the Israeli airforce's heavy losses

Top right **October: Somewhere in Sinai** a wounded man receives treatment

Top **13–19 October: A scene** during the greatest tank battle since the Second World War. Israeli Centurions wait in the shelter of a reverse slope before advancing

Above **10 October: Israeli tanks** wait to storm up the Golan Heights as the Israelis launched their comeback against Syria

Continued on following page

Gamma/Yves Del

The War day by day:

6 October: The Eygptian army crosses the Suez Canal at five points supported by USSR-made SAM-2 and SAM-3 missiles. Within 24 hours 400 Egyptian tanks had overrun the Bar Lev line. Syria launches a 1,400-tank attack across the Golan Heights, heavily outnumbering the Israeli forces

7 October: Egyptian Infantry reinforcements cross the canal and all forces push eastwards into the Sinai desert. Israeli Phantom jets strike at missile sites and canal crossings

6–10 October: Syrian forces advance 15 miles to the border of Israel proper. Rockets strike Israeli territory. Israelis bomb Damascus. Iraqi forces join Syrians

8 October: The whole East Bank of the canal falls into Egyptian hands.

9 October: Extensive tank battle takes place in Sinai. Egypt claims over 100 Israeli tanks destroyed

10 October: Israel launches strong counterattack on the Golan Heights

11 October: Israel overruns the Golan Heights. Syria claims the destruction of over 200 Israeli planes. Israel claims 800 Syrian tanks

12 October: Syrian forces are driven behind the 1967 ceasefire line into Syria proper. Israeli forces push towards Damascus

13 October: The last Israeli strong-point on the East Bank of the Suez Canal surrenders. Egyptian forces now 10 miles into Sinai

13–14 October: Advance on Damascus continues. Heavy Syrian resistance slows Israeli forces. Jordan and Saudi Arabia send troops to Syrian front

14 October: All Egyptain forces in Sinai — about 100,000 men — launch powerful armoured offensive

15 October: Iraqi forces on Syrian front are routed by Israelis, losing 250 tanks

14–19 October: Armoured battle rages in Sinai. More tanks are engaged than in the German invasion of Russia in 1941. Israeli air and armoured forces start to take toll of Egyptian tanks and missiles

15–22 October: Syrian resistance prevents further movement towards Damascus. Israelis reach Sasa, 20 miles from Damascus

17 October: An Israeli task force breaks through to establish a bridgehead on the West Bank

17–20 October: Bridgehead extended to 20 miles by 25. Israeli forces overrun or otherwise destroy all West Bank missile sites. Major counterattack in Sinai forces Egyptians back towards the canal

21 October: Israeli airforces now in total command of the skies on both fronts

22 October: UN-inspired ceasefire stops fighting on the Sinai front except in the area of the town of Suez where the Israelis fight on to surround the Egyptian 3rd Army, trapped east of the canal

23/24 October: Israel captures Mount Hermon in a helicopter-paratroop raid

24 October: Second UN ceasefire line agreed

Syria accepts UN ceasefire proposals

Rex Features

Rex Features

Rex Features

Rex Features

Popperfoto

Both pages October: **Golan Heights**. Israeli Centurion tanks recapture the town of Kuneitra — a town no more, having changed hands twice during the fighting

Top left October: **Golan Heights**. Jewish soldiers pray. If their subsequent success be any measure, their prayers were answered

Bottom left October: **Golan Heights**. Israeli tankmen duck as a Syrian aircraft hits the ground and explodes after being shot down by an Israeli fighter

Top right **7 October: Golan Heights**. The litter of retreat. The Syrian attack caught the Israelis unawares and forced them off these commanding heights overlooking Israel

Middle right October: **Suez Canal, West Bank**. A SAM-3 missile site captured in the Israeli bridgehead operation on the 17th

Bottom right October: **Suez**. Two Egyptian soldiers surrender as the Israelis surround the Egyptian 3rd Army

67

Press Association

Above **15 October: Edward Heath** shakes hands with Olafur Johannesson, Iceland's Prime Minister, to celebrate the end of the protracted and inglorious 'cod war' between Iceland and Britain. Their agreement banned 'freezer-factory' ships and limited the annual British catch to 130,000 tons

Right **October: The Cod War.** The cause of all the trouble – a netfull of cod and red mullet

Left **22 October: The greatest cellist dies.** Pablo Casals died at the great age of 96 after a career that brought him fame not only on the concert platform but throughout the world as a lover of liberty and a devoted opponent of all forms of totalitarianism. At the age of 87 he undertook a monumental world tour to promote the cause of international peace

Camera Press

Press Association

Above **31 October: The helicopter** used for Ireland's most brazen jail-break seen in Garda custody. Hired under false pretences, the helicopter was then hijacked and compelled to land in Mountjoy Jail yard. Prisoners formed a screen while Seamus Twomey, Kevin Mallon and Joe O'Hagan, all Provisional IRA leaders, were bundled into the helicopter and whisked away

Right **22 October: The scene in the** Spanish town of Murcia after floods that claimed over 500 lives in the south-west of Spain

Rex Features

Popperfoto

Associated Press

Left **17 October: Maynard Jackson** and his wife celebrate what ten years ago would have been impossible, his election as the first black mayor of a US southern city — Atlanta

Left **14 October: A helicopter** lowers a survivor from the capsized French dredger *Cap de la Hague* on to the rescue ship *Margaret*. Six men were trapped underneath the hull of the dredger for three days. Five died, but one, who managed to keep his head up in a pocket of air, survived

Pool Picture/Laurence Harris

1 & 2 Mr & Mrs Peter Phillips, 3 HRH Prince Edward, 4 Captain Eric Grounds, 5 Captain Mark Phillips, 6 HRH Princess Anne, 7 Lady Sarah Armstrong-Jones, 8 HRH Prince Charles, 9 HM The Queen, 10 HRH Prince Andrew, 11 HRH Prince Philip Duke of Edinburgh, 12 HM Queen Elizabeth Queen Mother

Rex Features

NOVEMBER

Far left **14 November: Princess Anne** poses with husband Captain Mark Phillips in Buckingham Palace shortly after their wedding

Top left **11 November: Five tiers** for the Royal Cake. Warrant-Officer David Dodd of the Army School for Catering puts the finishing touches to the cake, standing 5ft 8in high, which he designed and made himself. The cake weighed 145lb

Top right **14 November: HRH Princess Anne** stands on the balcony of Buckingham Palace with her husband of two hours, Captain Mark Phillips, surrounded by their in-laws. The Princess, who was 23, met her husband through their shared interest in horses

Left **14 November: The bridal** coach returns from Westminster Abbey to be cheered on its way to Buckingham Palace by the throngs of people lining the Mall

Rex Features

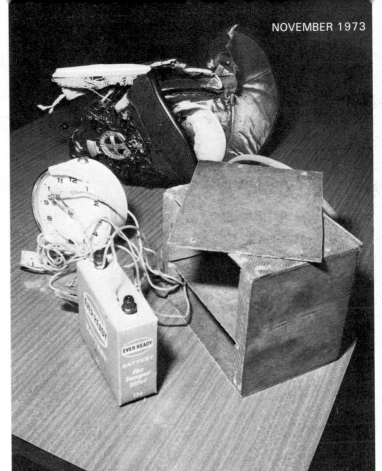

Press Association

Left **14 November: Miss Dolours Price,** 23, who, with her sister Marion, 20, and six others, was sentenced to life imprisonment for her part in IRA bombings outside the Old Bailey in March 1973. The trial was held at the Crown Court Winchester and lasted over two months. Stringent security precautions were taken and the Winchester police force was heavily reinforced by special squads from London. Attorney-General Sir Peter Rawlinson QC was prosecuting, assisted by Sir Joseph Maloney

Above **14 November: Exhibits from the** Old Bailey and Whitehall bomb blasts are shown at Winchester Crown Court trial: parts of one of the car bombs, which were responsible for the death of one person and the injury of 200, and the helmet of PC Malcolm Hine, who was severely injured by one of the blasts

Press Association

Above **1 November: Father Patrick Fell,** 32-year-old Roman Catholic priest, is found guilty of IRA activities and involvement in a bomb plot with five other men. Father Fell was arrested in April of 1973 and remanded in custody for eight days. Seven months later he was sentenced to 12 years' imprisonment

Rex Features

November: Arab-Israeli War. The aftermath. The ceasefire of 24 October left a perilously tense situation on both fronts. Israel permitted the supply of 'mercy' *materiel* to the beleaguered Egyptian 3rd Army, and UN ceasefire observers (largely from Cyprus, seriously weakening the UN presence in that other trouble spot) moved in along the canal front. Prolonged negotiations took place under UN auspices at Kilometre 101 on the Cairo—Suez road

Left **November 1973: Suez.** The UN observers move in

Below **November: Suez.** Israeli soldiers watch a UN relief column passing through their lines to the town of Suez

Gamma/Michel Laurent

Rex Features

Rex Features

Gamma

Middle **November 1973: Egypt** and Israel face each other across the conference table at Kilometre 101

Above **16 November: The ceasefire** agreement is finalised. Israeli and Egyptian officers shake hands

Gamma/Daniel Simon

Rex Features

Rex Features

17 November: Athens. Martial law is declared as students riot in Athens in protest against the Papadopoulos regime

Far left **19 November: Tank reinforcements** beam their searchlights on the Athens polytechnic as they join the assault. Twelve demonstrators were killed and more than 200 seriously injured in the street battles which raged throughout the night

Left **20 November:** The mangled debris of a wrecked car, railings and heavy piping bear witness to the violence of the fighting outside the Athens polytechnic. The students were demanding an end to the Papadopoulos regime, greater freedom in universities, resignation from NATO and the end of US influence in their country. Of the 866 demonstrators arrested, 391 were students

Left **24 November: President Papadopoulos** gives a press conference one day before the military coup which toppled him. Although the titular presidency had been his for only four months (since the deposal of the exiled King and Queen, seen in portraits above Papadopoulos) he had been the effective ruler of Greece since he took over from the Colonels. His rule had led to widespread dissatisfaction, expressed in the violent student riots of November. The military coup on the 25th was swift and bloodless and placed Papadopoulos under house arrest

Camera Press

Camera Press

In the aftermath of the Arab-Israeli war the Arab states made good their threat to reduce oil supplies to western nations. Faced with immediate oil shortages, Europe adopted emergency measures

Above **13 November: Garages were** shut with signs such as these throughout Britain from the middle of November onwards. The government ordered fuel deliveries to garages to be cut and, at the petrol stations which were open, queues formed dozens of cars long

Right **November: British shops were** ordered to use only such electricity as was essential, and all night advertising was banned by the government from 13 November

Far right top **2 November: Sunday driving** banned in Holland. The fast, modern Dutch motorways were empty of all cars, but bicycles were out in force on the side roads. The penalties were stringent enough to deter all but the most foolhardy: six months' imprisonment, a hefty fine, and confiscation of the car

Far right bottom **24 November: Horses** line the streets in Wild West fashion in Düsseldorf, Germany, after a Sunday driving ban came into force

Rex Features

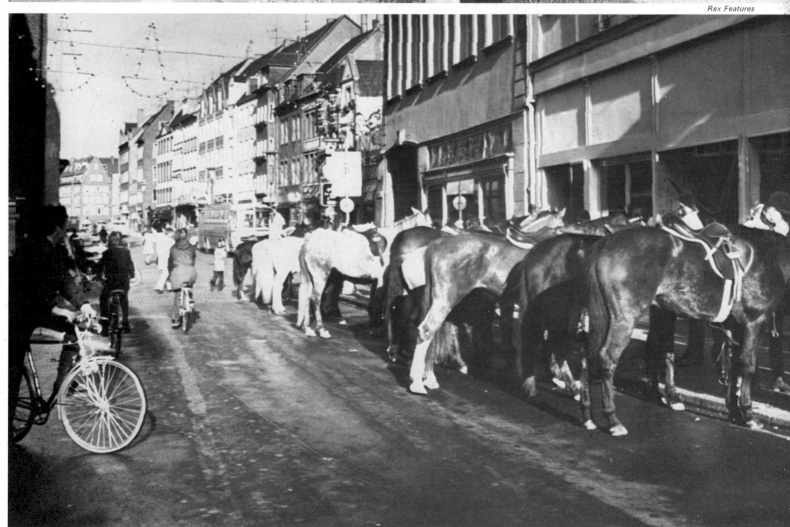

Popperfoto

1 November: Turkey, The impressive span of the Bosphorus Bridge is inaugurated by actor Danny Kaye. The £15m bridge, with a span of 1,074 metres, links Europe with Asia

John Hillelson/Thomas Hoepker

23 November: Moment of triumph for a new
Miss World. US contestant, Miss Marjorie Wallace
from Indianapolis, won the coveted crown for America
in the annual contest held in London in November

Associated Press

Left **17 November: Gerald Nabarro,** the flamboyant extrovert Conservative MP for Worcestershire South, dies at his home, aged 60. Sir Gerald had suffered three strokes within two months but had apparently made a good recovery. Three days before his death he had a fourth stroke and died without regaining consciousness. Sir Gerald was an entirely self-made man; in his army career he rose through the ranks from private to officer and in civilian life he started off as a labourer. Despite his dissatisfaction with his status as a 'mere' back-bencher, Sir Gerald succeeded in introducing some necessary reforms – the Clean Air Act in 1955 being one of them

Keystone

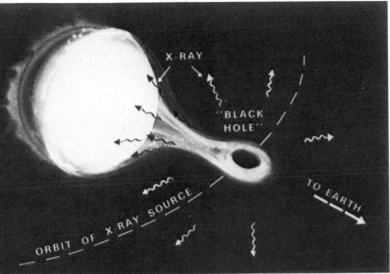

Left **24 November: X-rays taken from** the satellite, *Copernicus*, led to the reconstruction of this photograph of a 'black hole' star, six quadrillion miles from Earth. British scientists reported the first evidence to back up the theory that there are collapsed invisible stars — 'black holes' — in space. Astronomers in California also arrived at this conclusion, after separate research. 'Black holes' would be so dense and have such strong gravitational pull that even light could not escape from them — hence their invisibility

Associated Press

Popperfoto

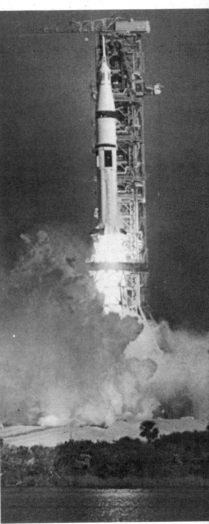

Popperfoto

Left **15 November: Members of the** Skylab 3 space mission on the eve of blast off: (*left to right*) William P. Pogue, Gerald P. Carr and Edward G. Gibson.

Above **16 November: Blast off** for the Saturn 1B rocket at Cape Canaveral which carried the Skylab 3 crew into orbit. The launching was successful for this, the longest, Skylab mission after suffering two delays when cracks in the rocket were discovered

85

Associated Press

Left **27 November: Rose Mary Woods,** President Nixon's private secretary of long-standing, at work. Miss Woods admitted before the Grand Jury of the Watergate trial that she could have 'accidentally' erased eighteen minutes from the crucial taped conversation between John Dean and the President while transcribing the tape. She claimed that while answering the telephone she pressed the 'record' button and kept her foot on the pedal throughout the telephone call. It was proved to the jury that to manage this feat she would have had to stretch over six feet across the room — this became known as the 'Rose Mary stretch!'

Above **26 November: Lieutenant-General** Phaedon Ghizikis the new Greek President emphasises a point at a cabinet session. Seated on his right is the Premier, Adamantios Androutsopoulos. The new constitution was determined to 'prepare the country for an undisturbed and genuinely democratic life'. The government did not want 'to establish a regime' or 'perpetuate the state of emergency'

Right **29 November: A killer fire** burns the Taiyo department store, Kumamoto, in southern Japan. The fire started on the third floor of the store and within minutes flames and smoke had spread throughout the seven storey building trapping hundreds of lunch-time shoppers. Many leapt to their death rather than be burnt to death or suffocated: 99 were killed and 100 injured

Below **27 November: A Dutch Boeing 747** stands at Malta's Luqa Airport with a full complement of 255 hostages on board. The Boeing was hijacked over Iraq by three Arab gunmen and forced to land on Malta. After negotiations the 247 passengers and eight stewardesses were released and the plane took off for an unnamed destination with the pilots under direction from the gunmen

Associated Press

Popperfoto

DECEMBER

2 December: Sir Alec Douglas Home, the British Foreign Secretary, is welcomed at Moscow at the start of his visit to the USSR. His talks with Andrei Gromyko, the Soviet Foreign Minister, covered the European Security Conference, mutual force reductions in Europe, the Middle East and Anglo-Soviet relations. The talks represented a thawing of relations that had been cold since Sir Alec's expulsion of 150 Soviet diplomats from Britain in 1971

Popperfoto

3 December: The US Space Probe *Pioneer 10* arrives at its closest point to the planet Jupiter and takes a series of photographs. This picture, taken from a distance of 1,614,000 miles, shows the famous 'red Spot' of Jupiter first observed in 1878 and more than 30,000 miles long. The banded markings are generally regarded as atmospheric phenomena, possibly caused by Jupiter's high rate of spin. The visible disc of Jupiter is very much larger than its actual bulk, the difference being explained by the very 'deep' atmosphere. *Pioneer 10*'s closest approach was to 88,700 miles

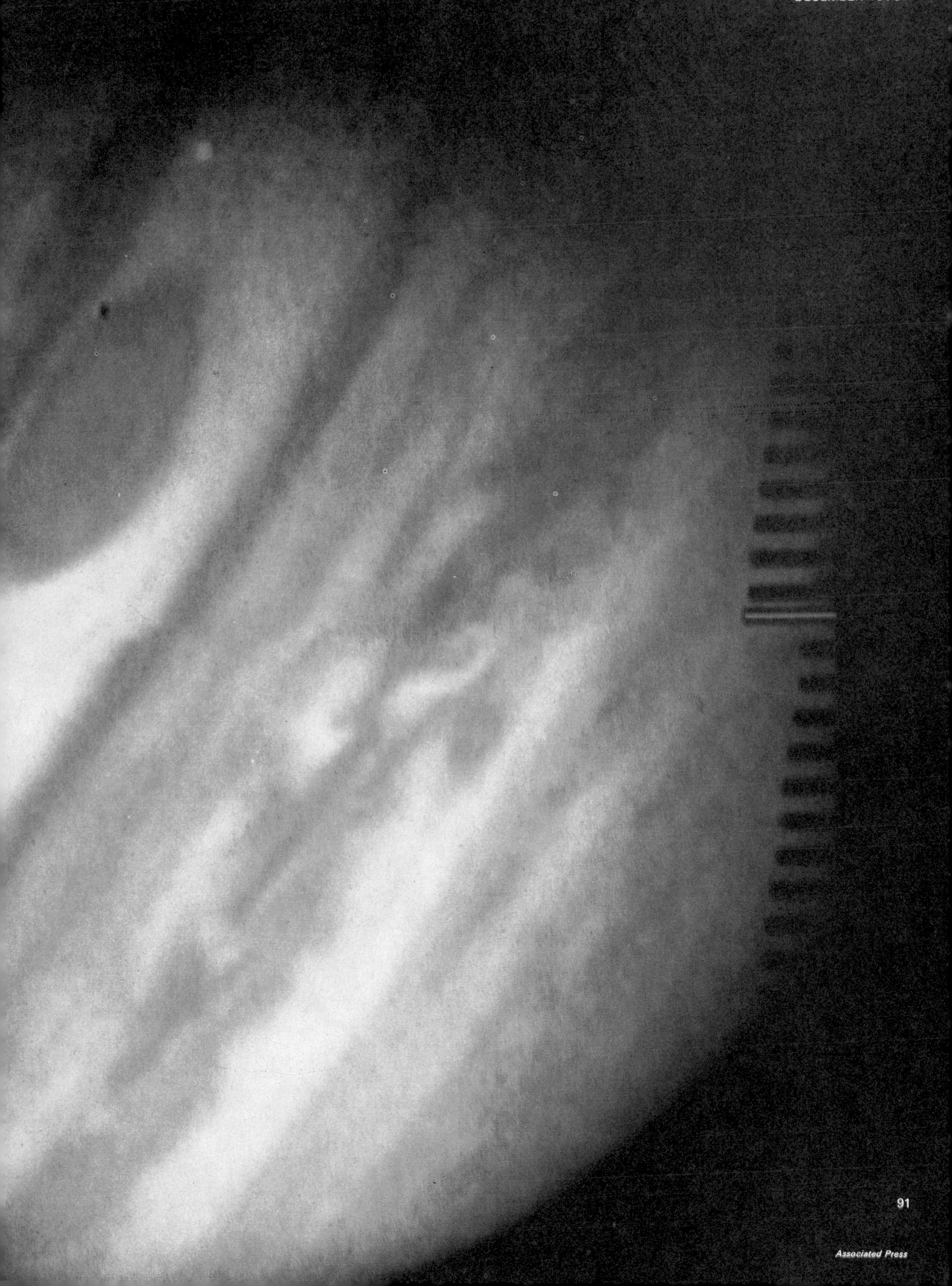

Associated Press

December: South Vietnam.
After the second Vietnam ceasefire on 15 June 1973, the scale of fighting (or, as they were euphemistically known, 'ceasefire violations') declined temporarily but intensified as the year came to an end. On 4 December the North Vietnamese, operating in Divisional strength for the first time since the ceasefire, captured Kien Duc in the Central Highland area. It was recaptured three days later. On 7 December South Vietnamese aircraft bombed targets in the Saigon sector, and more bombing was carried out in the Mekong Delta on the 17th. On the 25th Government troops and NLF forces became engaged in heavy fighting in the Mekong Delta resulting in a three-day battle

Right **13 December: Villagers** flee with their most prized possession, a working elephant, from the fighting in the Central Highlands

Below **14 December: Government** troops dig in as a transport plane flies supplies into Kien Duc

Associated Press

Associated Press

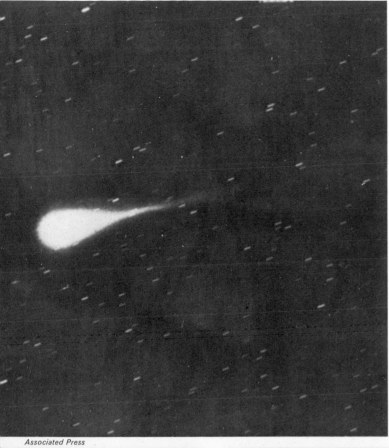

Associated Press

Sotheby & Co

Above **5 December: The Cubist** painting by Picasso, *Femme Assise*, fetches the record price of £340,000 on auction at Sotheby's, London

Associated Press

Above left **4 December: The first good** glimpse of the comet Kohoutek seen through the telescopes of the Hale observatories on Palomar Mountain, California. Forecast by astronomers to brighten the night skies of December and January, Kohoutek turned out to be something of a disappointment, providing no Halley-like display

Left **12 December: The comet's discoverer,** Lubos Kohoutek, chats to George Halley, descendant of another famous comet's discoverer. Both were guests on board the *QE 2* on a trip to secure a good look at the comet Kohoutek

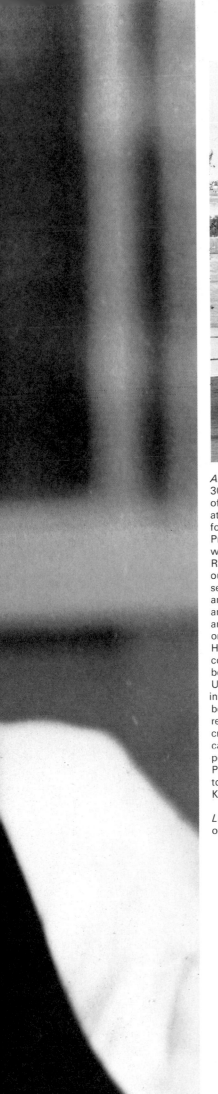

Rex Features

Above **1 December: Some of the** 300,000 who filed past the coffin of David Ben Gurion lying in state at the Knesset, Jerusalem. The founder of Israel and her first Prime Minister, Gurion was 87 when he died. Born at Plonsk in Russian Poland, he was from the outset a passionist Zionist. He settled in Palestine when only 20 and was involved in many socialist and trade union movements. During and after the Second World War he organised the secret movement, the Haganah, to defend the Jewish community against the Arabs, and became Prime Minister when the UN partition of Palestine was put into force in 1948. With a break between 1953 and 1955 he remained in office until the Suez crisis in 1956 when Israeli forces captured and held the Sinai peninsula. He remained active in Politics until 1969, when he retired to spend the rest of his life on a Kibbutz in the Negev desert

Left **David Ben Gurion** pictured on his 86th birthday

Rex Features

Above: **15 December. Paul Getty junior** is released by his kidnappers. Held since 10 July, Getty was returned without his right ear, severed by his kidnappers after the Italian police had seemed reluctant to take the case seriously, and after the boy's grandfather, one of the richest men in the world, had refused to pay the ransom. Eventually the senior Getty paid a ransom rumoured to be almost £1m, the largest non-political, one-person ransom ever paid

Right **14 December: President Sadat** of Egypt announces changes in his army command following the disasters on the Sinai front in late October

Popperfoto

14 December: Sadat's new nominees. Major-General Gamassy (*above*) became Chief-of-Staff, and Major-General Badawi (*below*) took over the 3rd Army, whose previous commander had allowed it to be trapped on the wrong side of the Great Bitter Lake in the October fighting

Popperfoto

Gamma/J. P. Bonnotte

December 1973: A youngster gazes at the announcement of a performance by Uri Geller. During the last part of 1973, Geller rode the crest of one of those waves of public credibility not uncommon in the west. Claiming to be able to perform various feats by psychic power alone, Geller, a young Israeli, broke steel objects, copied sealed drawings, drove cars blindfold, and levitated objects. Armed with an engagingly frank personality, Geller seemed honest and unpretentious about his powers, and his fame and popularity grew. During TV appearances viewers phoned in to report that all their cutlery had bent, and the Institute of Scientific Research at Stamford University, California, conducted an investigation of his claims, cautiously claiming that they could find no evidence of conjuring or sleight of hand. But as the volume of adulation grew, other voices were heard. Long-standing professional magicians came forward to explain, not how it was done, but that they could do it too. A British journalist offered an explanation of the spoon-bending: a simple household chemical (too dangerous, he said, to name in case children should use it) rubbed on the fingers weakened the spoon and caused it to break when rubbed.

Although his name faded out of the headlines, much of Geller's magic remained unexplained. More rigorous tests were needed to show whether Geller was using unexplained powers or whether he was merely a very skilled conjurer

Press Association

Above **Geller** holds up the results of his efforts in his London hotel

Rex Features/David McEnery

Right **14 December: In spite of top level** meetings of the leaders of the nine EEC member countries, the Community failed to present a united or firm front to the Arab nations during the last two months of 1973 as the Arab oil cut-down began to pinch the west's economy. Following this meeting, on the 15th, a compromise was reached which agreed in vague terms to share the Community's oil supplies on an equal basis, and to conduct joint research into oil substitutes. The Arabs were later neatly to undermine this unity by increasing supplies to most member countries, but continuing to 'black' Holland, considered by the Arabs to be the arch 'pro-Israeli' western nation

Left **December: A refinery** in Libya 'burning off'. The hard line taken by the Arab nations over oil was to some extent dictated by their realisation that, with the development of other oilfields and other technologies, their stranglehold would not continue indefinitely

Popperfoto

Sygma/J. Daune

Above **17 December: A Tokyo stock exchange clerk** tries to keep pace with the rapid fluctuations of stock caused by the oil crisis. Perhaps hardest hit of all the industrial countries, Japan's 1973 trade figures showed a record £740m deficit for the month of November

Right **December: Tokyo.** An exhortation to the Japanese people to save energy. With 40% of her fuel imports from Arab states Japan's crisis by the end of the year was acute, and the Vice-Minister for Trade and Industry said that the economy was facing collapse

Rex Features

Sygma/J. Daune

Associated Press

Above **17 December: An injured man,** hit by bullets and glass fragments, tries to rise. He was among the 40 killed and 18 injured at Rome Airport when Arab guerrillas launched a terror attack, firing at waiting passenger queues and throwing fire bombs into a crowded jet waiting on the runway. Their attack was timed to coincide with the trial in Italy of Arabs accused of plotting to shoot down an Israeli aircraft with rockets in 1972

Left **17 December: The burnt-out** fuselage of the Pan Am jet in which 30 people died strapped in their seats as the terrorists flung fire bombs into the plane

Below **18 December:** Two of the five Arab terrorists give victory salutes after their massacre at Rome Airport. They had hijacked another aircraft and flown to Kuwait. There they surrendered to the authorities

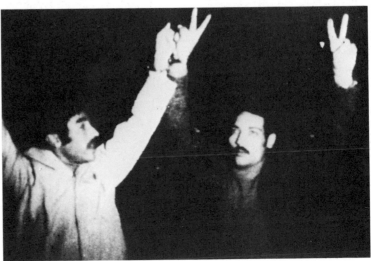

Sygma/Patric Morin   Popperfoto

Right **2 December: William Whitelaw** becomes Secretary of State for Employment. Edward Heath's cabinet reshuffle in December came at a time when Whitelaw had succeeded in arranging tripartite talks on the future of Ireland. His removal to the Ministry of Employment was seen as an attempt to bring his formidable negotiating powers to bear on Britain's worsening industrial situation

Below **12 December: Thousands of angry commuters** wait to get home at London's Liverpool Street Station in what had become almost an annual celebration of one of the greatest absurdities of the British industrial scene — a work to rule. On the 12th the members of ASLEF embarked, not on a strike, but on a strict adherence to the safety regulations of their job. So widely were these disregarded that their mere application caused rail chaos. The ASLEF members imposed their work to rule at a time when mineworkers were taking the same action, and the economy was facing grave difficulties because of the fuel crisis. One facet of the work to rule was the blow it dealt to the image of the English commuter as sang-froid in a bowler hat. At some London stations police had to intervene to save ASLEF members from enraged commuters

Associated Press

Popperfoto

Sygma/Selwyn Tait

Above **9 December: All smiles as the Tripartite** Sunningdale talks on the future of Ireland meet with success. Liam Cosgrave, the Eire Premier, shakes hands with Brian Faulkner, the Chief Executive Designate of Northern Ireland. The Sunningdale agreement set up a Council of Ireland, with representatives from North and South, and a Northern Ireland Executive. Time was to show, however, that no one at the conference had truly represented the wishes of the majority of the Ulster protestants, and the agreement was doomed to a short life

Right **18 December: Police** pick over the wreckage of a car bomb outside London's Pentonville prison. Five people were hurt in the explosion, one of several that injured a total of 60 people. The wave of bombings was believed to be an attempt by the Provisional IRA to secure the transfer of their members convicted of the 1972 London bombings from prison in England to Northern Ireland

Popperfoto

Popperfoto

Above **20 December:** These two pictures show clearly the force of the explosion that killed the Spanish Prime Minister, Admiral Carrero Blanco, as his car returned from Mass in Madrid. The bomb, planted by a Basque separatist group, the ETA, hurled the Prime Minister's two-ton car over 65-ft high buildings

Right **21 December: The US Vice-President,** Gerald Ford (hatless) attends Carrero's funeral. The Admiral had been increasingly presiding over Cabinet meetings in the place of General Franco (arrowed). Indeed a communiqué from the Basque ETA movement stated that the admiral had been assassinated because he 'guaranteed the continuity of the Franco regime'

Gamma/Cosmos

JANUARY

9 January: **Mstislav Rostropovich**, the celebrated Soviet cellist, plays in Beethoven's *The Trio of the Archduke* accompanied by pianist Wilhelm Kempff and violinist Yehudi Menuhin. Rostropovich was banned from leaving Russia for three years for his public defence of dissident novelist Alexander Solzhenitsyn. He was allowed to leave the USSR to play in a Gala concert given at the Paris Salle Pleyel on the occasion of the 25th Anniversary of the International Council of Music.

Camera Press

Above **January: Work continues** at this coal mine in Wales but the overtime ban had severely cut production

Right **January: Machinery is still** during an overtime period at this coal mine on a Sunday

Camera Press

Camera Press

Above **January: Coal miners** during their waiting time. To be paid for these 'waiting' periods would still have failed to meet the union's demands

January: The UK Mineworkers' dispute reached its crisis, and ended in a pithead ballot to strike, in January 1974. The government had stood firm on its decision not to treat mineworkers as a special case, and the Coal Board made an offer within the limits of the Phase III counter-inflationary structure. The offer was rejected by the miners and by 12 November 1973 the NUM decided to put a ban on overtime working. Output was drastically reduced and this, coupled with the oil crisis and industrial action by electricity workers, led to the government's declaring a State of Emergency. At the beginning of January it was hoped that a decision could be reached by paying miners money for their waiting time: this would include gathering equipment, journeys to and from the coal face and time spent washing and changing at the end of each shift. It was discovered that money paid for the additional time would still fall far short of the NUM's requirements. Mr Len Murray, General Secretary of the TUC, offered his assurances to the government that if the miners were treated as a special case he would ensure that other unions would not use that as an argument for their own settlements. This proposal was rejected by the Chancellor of the Exchequer, Anthony Barber, and further talks ended in deadlock. On

25 January the NUM gave warning to the NCB that a national strike might be called from midnight on 9 February if the ballot was 55% in favour. Alleged communist influence within the NUM executive was sternly criticised and Mick McGahey, the NUM Vice-President, came under heavy attack. The Ballot took place on 31 January and showed an overwhelming 80·99% vote in favour of a national strike

Right **9 January: Leaders of the NUM** (left to right) Vice-President Mick McGahey, President Joe Gormley and General Secretary Lawrence Daly arrive at the Department of Employment for talks with Employment Secretary Mr William Whitelaw

Popperfoto

Below **12 January: Mgr Serafeim,** the Bishop of Janina, arrives at the Holy Synod's building in Athens after his election by 20 votes to eight to the Primacy of Greece

Rex Features

Popperfoto

Associated Press

Right: **24 January: Miners demonstrate** outside the NUM's headquarters during a meeting between the three leaders of the NUM and the union's 27-man executive to discuss a possible strike ballot of the union's 260,000 members

Rex Features

Left **7 January: A scene in** the suburbs of Phnom Penh after the attack by 3,000 Khmer Rouge insurgents which brought fighting up to the city limits. The town itself suffered heavily from rocket and mortar attacks. This was the heaviest attack on the town itself for almost six months

Above **7 January: The work of** a single mortar bomb falling in a crowded street

Popperfoto

Above **11 January: Rome firemen** survey the damage caused by one of four bombs which exploded in the offices of an Italian Insurance Company connected with the American Corporation ITT (International Telephone and Telegraph Corporation). The bombs, which exploded within a few minutes of each other just after midnight, caused substantial damage but no one was injured. Pamphlets were scattered around the building, accusing ITT of organising a 'fascist and reactionary' plot in Italy by means of telephone tapping. The pamphlets also accused ITT of being responsible for the coup in Chile (see September 1973)

Right **15 January: Empty railway tracks** near Victoria Station, London, bear witness to the stoppage caused by a 24-hour strike. Five days before the ASLEF union had ended its policy of non-co-operation, but the one-day strike went ahead because British Rail would not agree to further talks on pay 'restructuring'. Commuters were left stranded on crowded platforms for hours, and most were forced to find alternative methods of transport

Popperfoto

Popperfoto

Below **7 January: An armoured vehicle stands guard** at London's Heathrow Airport which was put on full military alert in an anti-terrorist operation

Left **7 January: A policeman,** backed up by troops and a Saracen armoured car, orders a passenger to open his luggage for a search. The massive alert mounted by troops and police lasted several days and the security was redoubled for the arrival of the new Israeli Ambassador in London, Mr Gideon Rafael. It was feared that terrorists might launch an attack with small, man-portable, anti-aircraft SAM missiles. However, no incident occurred

Associated Press

Associated Press

Rex Features

Above **28 January: The melan-choly view** of Brisbane, Australia, after the territory had experienced devastating floods following years of prolonged drought. At least 40 suburbs were inundated, and the city's life disrupted on a vast scale. The phenomenon of 'affluent looting' — men in power boats robbing flooded homes — made its appearance. With 8,000 homeless, and a damage bill of hundreds of millions of pounds, the State of Queensland faced its worst crisis ever

Above right **1 January: Victor Feather,** the former General Secretary of the TUC, celebrates the news of his life peerage with a cigar. Vic Feather was assistant general secretary of the TUC for nine years before he became secretary, a position held for four years until his retirement in the autumn of 1973. He was succeeded by his assistant secretary, Mr Len Murray

Right **28 January: The Greek** ambassador to Cyprus lays a wreath on the deathbed of General George Grivas, who died on the 27th. Grivas fought all his life for Enosis, the union of Cyprus with Greece, first against the British and then against his own countrymen under President Makarios, earning a reputation of one of the doughtiest guerrilla leaders of the century

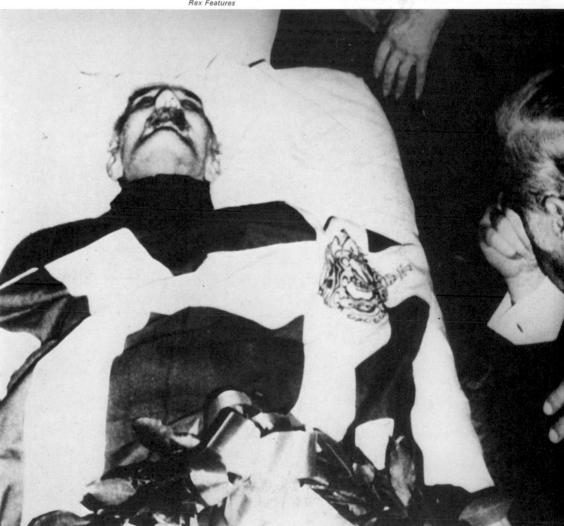

Associated Press

112

Associated Press

Left **7 January: Japanese Prime Minister Kakuei Tanaka** before the start of his tour of five South East Asian countries

Below **9 January: Thai student demonstrators** set fire to a model of a Japanese car in protest against 'Japanese economic imperialism'. Thousands of students turned out to picket the Bangkok airport on Tanaka's arrival and many more mobbed his hotel waving banners saying 'Imperialist Monster Tanaka' and shouting 'Get out you ugly imperialist'. Police forced a path through the mob to get the Prime Minister to his hotel

UPI

Associated Press

Above **16 January: An Indonesian youth is clubbed** into unconsciousness by an army trooper while resisting arrest. Growing antagonism towards the big Japanese business concerns, which were forcing smaller Indonesian companies out of production, culminated in serious riots during Japanese Prime Minister Tanaka's visit to Jakarta

Right **16 January: Indonesian troops** attempt to keep the throngs of students milling through the streets in check. Ten thousand students ran riot through Jakarta destroying every Japanese car in sight and burning the Toyota car offices to the ground in their war against Japanese 'imperialism and exploitation'. Police opened fire during the riots, killing eight people and injuring 36

John Hillelson

Right **7 January: Brian Faulkner** announces his resignation of the leadership of the Unionist Party in Northern Ireland and his intention of remaining at the head of the week-old Ulster Executive. Eighteen other Unionists resigned with him and announced their intention of setting up a reconstituted party loyal to Mr Faulkner and his involvement in the Sunningdale agreement and the principle of power-sharing. His resignation followed a vote of no confidence by the Unionist members in the Ulster Assembly

Below **22 January: Mr John Dunlop,** Assembly member for mid-Ulster (Bernadette Devlin's former constituency), is evicted from the Assembly by police after he and other Unionists had made good their threat to sabotage its first sitting. Their tactics included filibustering, shouting, and fighting

Popperfoto

Popperfoto

114

Above **22 January: A policeman** arrests a woman striker near a textile factory in Durban, South Africa. Disturbances occurred after a peaceful walkout by textile workers, and the police were called in

Right **29 January: Herbert Ernest Bates CBE**, the 68-year-old novelist, playwright and short story writer, dies in a Canterbury hospital. H. E. Bates, as he was known, was a prolific writer with over 50 books to his credit. He published his first novel, *The Two Sisters*, aged 20. Bates wrote his best work when inspired by his own experiences, either in the RAF as with *Fair Stood the Wind for France*, or in the English countryside. Bates probably reached his widest audience with his novels of life with the Larkin family; *The Darling Buds of May* was the first of a series of best sellers. Bates had much of his best work televised in the Granada Television series, *Country Matters*, and in 1970 his novella *The Triple Echo* was published and made into a successful film. H. E. Bates married in 1931 and had four children

22 January: Sioux warriors pictured during the 'siege' of Wounded Knee during 1973. On 22 January Indians turned out in force to vote at the polls in the Wounded Knee area of South Dakota to show their feelings about the takeover of their settlement in 1973. The two main candidates are Mr Russell Means, one of the leaders of the militant American Indian Movement, and Mr Richard Wilson, President of the tribal council. During the siege Mr Wilson had threatened to break through the federal agents' lines surrounding Wounded Knee and eject the occupiers himself. White reporters on the scene were unable to judge the progress of the Indians campaign efforts

Right **25 January: Israeli soldiers** clear mines preparatory to evacuating the West Bank positions gained in the October war. The US and USSR sponsored Geneva peace conference, and the talks at Kilometre 101, had produced an agreement for the disengagement of Arab and Israeli forces on the Suez Canal front by 17 January. The agreement allowed for a limited Egyptian presence on the East Bank and the withdrawal of Israeli forces to a line approximately 10–20 miles east of the canal

Below **January 1974: Syria.** Having boycotted the Geneva conference, the Syrian government was not party to the disengagement agreement. An Israeli tank crew, more accustomed to the heat of the desert, sit out the winter on their ceasefire lines on Mount Hermon

Popperfoto

Associated Press

January 1974: The lull after the storm. An Israeli soldier takes his rest on a shattered gun emplacement overlooking the Gulf of Eilat

Rex Features

Associated Press

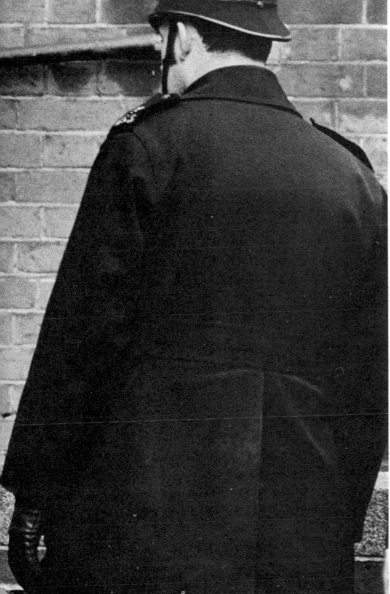

Above **31 January: Samoa. The burnt-out shell** of the Pan American Boeing 707, which crashed in a violent thunderstorm, lies crumpled a quarter of a mile from Pago Pago Airport. Ninety-four people were killed. The pilot sent out a message shortly before the crash saying that the plane was on fire. It came down in a banana and breadfruit plantation and burst into flames. Many would-be survivors were trapped inside and burnt to death. Only eight people managed to get out alive

Left **29 January: Miss Alison Thompson,** an 18-year-old model, is escorted into court during her trial for conspiring to possess weapons illegally. The American girl and her two guerrilla friends, Pakistani Ather Naseem, 21, and Moroccan Abdelkbir El-Hakkaoui, the 25-year-old leader of the group, were believed to be part of an organisation plotting to kidnap or kill the Moroccan Ambassador in London. The three were arrested at London's Heathrow Airport while attempting to smuggle arms and ammunition into the country. Special Branch detectives could find no evidence that the group had any connection with either the Black September terrorists or any other Palestinian Liberation group

Sygma/Selwyn Tait

Associated Press

Above **31 January: A soldier** stands guard outside a workmen's hut whose occupants, having a lunch-break game of cards, had been mown down by gunmen a few hours before. The men were employed at a cable laying site at Newtonabbey near Belfast. Two were killed and three wounded

Right **31 January: The interior** of the hut after the murders. The gunmen burst in and shot the men at their game of cards. The company concerned employed labour on a non-sectarian basis, and it was assumed that sectarian feeling was the motive for the killings

Associated Press

120

FEBRUARY

14 February: Alexander Solzhenitsyn, the dissident Soviet novelist exiled from his country on 12 February, holds a press conference at the home of fellow writer and Nobel-prizewinner, Heinrich Böll, in Langenbroich, West Germany. Solzhenitsyn was stripped of his Soviet citizenship and sent to West Germany after the publication of his most recent book *The Gulag Archipelago*. He claimed that while under arrest in Moscow he was threatened with the death penalty for treason. Solzhenitsyn later left West Germany for Zurich where he was joined by his wife and four children after they were allowed out of the USSR (see page 150)

Associated Press

Rex Features

Rex Features

Left **4 February: Berkeley, California.** Patricia Hearst, daughter of publishing millionaire Randolph Hearst, pictured here with her fiancé, Stephen Weed, was kidnapped from her apartment by masked black men. Weed was beaten in his attempts to foil the kidnappers, and several shots were fired at neighbours who tried to help. Half-naked, Patricia was bundled into the boot of a car and driven away. Later a group styled the Symbionese Liberation Army claimed responsibility and demanded that Hearst distribute $2m of food to the needy. On 21 February they trebled this demand to $6m, almost £3m. The kidnappers communicated by tape recordings

Below **17 February: Nominated by** the kidnappers as intermediaries for the food distribution were (*left to right*) Yvonne Golden of the Black Teachers' Caucus; the Rev Cecil Williams, Pastor of the Glide Memorial Methodist Church; and Dennis Banks of the American Indian movement

Above **4 February: The distraught** Hearst parents hold a press conference after the kidnapping

Below **21 February: Food supplies** are prepared for distribution as Randolph Hearst complied with the kidnappers' demands

Associated Press

Popperfoto

16 February: Thomas Gatch checks his wireless before embarking on an Atlantic crossing. Seen wearing high-altitude clothing, he is in the gondola which, supported by 10 helium balloons, he hoped would carry him from Harrisburg Airport, Pennsylvania, to southern Europe or Africa

Gamma/David Burnett

Rex Features

6 February: Paris. If elephants could fly, the Anglo-French Concorde might qualify as the greatest white elephant ever. On the 6th a report by French experts advocated three major alterations to the already drastically expensive project. The alterations were needed to increase range, reduce noise and improve aerodynamic performance

9/10 February: Britain's mine-workers strike Following the failure of the miners' overtime ban (declared in November) to win their pay demands, a ballot was held among the mineworkers' union members on 1 February to authorise the union to call a national strike. The ballot showed an overwhelming 'yes', and the strike was called for midnight on the 9/10th. It was a body blow to Edward Heath's Conservative government's attempts to nurse an economy already stricken by the miners' overtime ban, a similar ban by electrical engineers and above all the drop in oil imports. Britain, already working on a three-day week, faced the prospect of imminent 'energy starvation'. Widespread public sympathy for the miners as a specially deserving case in the wage queue was offset by the spectacle of their ruthless unconcern for the rest of the community at a time of national crisis, and many fears were roused by the political objectives announced (unofficially) by some of the more extreme union members

Associated Press

Right **The job that no one wants to do.** The dirt and danger of coal-mining show on the face of this collier from the Welsh coalfields

Far right **10 February: Joe Gormley,** President of Britain's National Union of Mineworkers, gives a press conference

Below **Miners in the lift** that will take them down for their eight-hour shift on the coal face

Camera Press

Associated Press

Rex Features

Associated Press

Above **Miners picket a power station** to prevent deliveries of coal. Picketing during the strike was orderly and peaceful

Left **A miner from Aberfan,** Cledwyn Thomas, lends his back for his friends to fill in their ballot papers voting to strike

Right **Students demonstrate** their solidarity with the miners' cause

Rex Features

Gamma/Michel Laurent

Above **6 February: The decks of** the wrecked Saudi Arabian cargo ship, the *Star of Shaddia*, are littered with the pitiful corpses of some of the 12,000 sheep, cows and camels left aboard to die when the ship went aground in heavy weather on the deserted island of Djebel Zebair. A few survivors continue the hopeless quest for food

Gamma/Michel Laurent

Right **6 February: Stoical camels** await death by thirst and starvation

Below **6 February: The battered** *Star of Shaddia* takes further punishment from the angry sea

Gamma/Michel Laurent

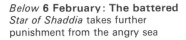

Right **27 February: M. Pierre Messmer** faces the press after an interview with President Pompidou at the Elysée Palace. On the morning of the 27th M. Messmer handed in the resignation of his Cabinet to the President. But when the new Prime Ministerial appointment was announced by the Elysée Palace it was none other than M. Messmer again. The decision took everyone, except the President and the Premier, by surprise. Obviously the object was to pave the way for a drastic Cabinet reshuffle in order to face France's growing economic problems and energy crisis. M. Michel Jobert and M. Valery Giscard d'Estaing were expected to keep their key positions as Foreign and Finance Ministers

Associated Press

Right **1 February: Muhammad Hassanein Heykal,** the editor of the foremost Egyptian newspaper and the most powerful information medium in the country *Al Ahram*, is removed from his position by President Sadat. Mr Heykal was the last voice of Nasserism in President Sadat's regime and his removal to the post of 'presidential adviser on press affairs' seemed to indicate a new period of 'de-Nasserisation' throughout Egypt. The new editor, Mr Ali Amin, started off on the wrong foot with the paper's staff — all recruited by Mr Heykal — by saying, when asked what he was going to do, that he had only had time to give the paper 'underclothes' and that he was preparing to dress it in its 'bridal gown'. He later gave a television interview retracting this statement

Camera Press

Below **20 February: Mrs Golda Meir** announces in Tel Aviv that she undertakes to form Israel's first minority Government, holding 58 seats of the 120-seat Knesset. This coalition of the 51 members of the Labour Alignment Party, four Independent Liberals and three Arabs, ended a seven-week Cabinet crisis. The National Religion Party, which held ten seats, withdrew from negotiations on the eve of Mrs Meir's decision and combined with the right-wing Likud and Tora Religious Front to hold 54 seats. The deciding seats were the four new Communist-held seats, the three Civil Rights Lists seats, and the one seat held by the left-wing Moked Party — but it seemed unlikely that any of these members would side with the right-wing opposition. Mr Moshe Dayan, the former Defence Minister, was expected to be included in the new Cabinet

Rex Features

11/12 February: Khmer Republic. Phnom Penh burns after another devastating attack by encircling rebel forces. The rebels, firing captured US 105mm howitzers, poured an estimated 73 shells into crowded market and residential areas of the city. More than 1,000 homes were destroyed as fires took hold. The area hit was only a few hundred yards from the President's Palace, and it was assumed that this was the intended target. The dead numbered 140, and over 200 were injured

Below **11 February: Carnage** in Phnom Penh's street market

Gamma/John Giannini

Above **12 February: The fires burn on** and the homeless rescue their few possessions as street life returns to normal after the bombardment

Rex Features

Rex Features

Gamma/Serge Limoine

Gamma/Serge Limoine

Above **February: The Queen,** Prince Philip, Princess Anne and Captain Mark Phillips find time for relaxation during their royal visit to New Zealand, Papua New Guinea and the New Hebrides

Left **25 February: The Queen** is escorted through Goroka Park, Headquarters of the Eastern Highlands of Papua New Guinea, to watch the tribal dances. Behind her stand Princess Anne, Prince Philip and Captain Mark Phillips. More than 6,000 warriors from all over the island came to welcome her and to watch the dancing. The Queen exchanged gifts with all the tribal chiefs after the celebrations had finished

Magnum/Phillip Jones Griffiths

Left **February 1974: British soldiers** 'sniff' for concealed gelignite in the sewers of Londonderry

Below **12 February: A crowd of** police and service officers gathers in the grounds of the Latimer National Defence College after a bomb, planted by the Provisional IRA, had injured 10 people. The defence college was one of many 'soft' military targets in England hit by the IRA during 73/74. Training camps and colleges, being lightly defended but yet military installations, made excellent targets for bombers increasingly hampered in Ireland, by military operations in the north, and by less and less sympathetic attitudes in the south.

Press Association

Popperfoto

Above **15 February: Dungannon, N Ireland.** The main square of Dungannon after the explosion of what may have been the largest bomb ever to be detonated in Ulster. A post-office van, containing an estimated 700lb of explosive, was placed in the square by masked men. In spite of the size of the explosion there were no casualties

Gamma/David Burnett

Above **6/7 February: Grenada. Two British marines** lower the Union Jack at midnight on the 6/7th as Grenada became independent. The ceremonics were slightly marred by the state of unrest in Grenada as middle-class and radical elements joined in an uneasy alliance to oppose independence under Eric Gairy, the island's Prime Minister. Strikes and other protests brought the island to a standstill. Gairy's opponents feared that the Caribbean island might become another Haiti under Gairy's personal dictatorship. His 'Mongoose Squad' corresponded closely to the infamous 'Tonton Macoute' of Haiti

Left **4 February: Rio de Janeiro.** Great train robber, Ronald Biggs, puts a grateful arm around his Brazilian girlfriend Raimunda de Castro. Miss de Castro had come forward to claim that she was pregnant by Biggs, a claim that could have led to his detention in Brazil in spite of Britain's plea for his extradition to complete his 30-year jail sentence

Popperfoto

Gamma/Michel Laurent

Left **21 February: Israeli troops grin** and wave victory signs as they cross to the East Bank of the canal 129 days after occupation began. At noon the Israeli flag was lowered on the West Bank by the same man who had raised it in October. UN forces held the canal road bridge for six hours before Egyptian troops moved in and they remained as a buffer on the canal banks until the Israeli troops completed withdrawal through the UN zone to their new position, 13 miles east of the canal, decided in the disengagement agreement negotiated by Dr Henry Kissinger

Above **February: Syrian-held Israeli prisoners** sit, hands clasped behind their heads. February saw an exchange of Arab and Israeli POWs, but the situation was complicated by the Syrian refusal to publish lists of those captured

Above right **21 February: Rejoicing Israeli troops** do a 'Hora' dance across the canal. In the background the explosions of champagne corks, not gunfire, could be heard. Horns blared, red flares were ignited and from one lorry a flock of doves was released to commemorate the deaths of all the young Israeli soldiers who fought in the Yom Kippur war

Right **28 February: Moshe Dayan** grips the hand of a mourner at a memorial service for Israel's unknown soldiers at Mt Herzl military cemetery. When he spoke to give comfort and support to the bereaved some chanted back 'Dayan, murderer. Dayan, murderer'

Gamma/Michel Laurent

Press Association   *Popperfoto*

28 February: Britain goes to the polls in the closest-fought and most contentious election of her recent history. Faced with the prospect of economic breakdown, brought on by oil shortages, industrial action in the power industry and on the railways, and the national strike of Britain's coalminers (see page 124), Edward Heath's Conservative government had no alternative but to call a general election to put to the electorate its determination to continue the Phase 3 counter-inflationary policy. The election was announced on the 7th, to take place on the 28th, and from the start wages and industrial relations dominated the campaign. In the background hovered the Industrial Relations Act, the Conservative's attempt to make Trade Unions answerable to some form of contractual law, a much-hated and misunderstood piece of legislation to whose overthrow the unions and the Labour Party were dedicated.

Throughout the campaign the result was in doubt. Not only did opinion polls forecast an almost neck and neck position for the main parties, but many of the constituencies had been altered since the previous election, making accurate prediction impossible. The final result was, in fact, confusingly inconclusive. Labour 301 seats, Conservatives 296, Liberals 14, Scottish Nationalists 7, Welsh Nationalists 2, Independent Labour 1, Democratic Labour 1, United Ulster Unionists 11, and Social Democratic and Labour Party 1. With only five seats separating them the two main parties were bound to look for support among the other major seat holders and, looking, found important blocks held by such disparate elements as Liberals, Scottish Nationalists and Ulstermen. The scene was set for multi-party rule on European lines

Below **14 February: Conservative leader** Edward Heath addresses party loyalists at an electioneering rally in Birmingham. Up to the last moment opinion polls showed a slight Conservative lead over Labour, and in terms of votes polled they were right. The Conservative Party polled 11,928,677 votes against Harold Wilson's Labour Party's 11,661,488. But in terms of Parliamentary seats Labour had the edge, with 301 to 296

Associated Press

Far left **7 February: Commuters** at London's Charing Cross, waiting for trains delayed by the railmen's industrial action, read the news of the pending election

Left **23 February: Tory maverick** Enoch Powell gestures during an anti-election, anti-Common Market speech in Birmingham. Powell resigned his seat when the election was announced, calling it 'fraudulent'. He advocated that his supporters should vote Labour in order to get Britain out of the Common Market. Of all the acts in his long career of baiting the leaders of his own party, this was the one most closely resembling political suicide

Below left **12 February: A meditative** pipe for Labour's Harold Wilson as he listens to a question at a Party press conference. Labour's fortunes fluctuated during the campaign and they faced a challenge not only from the Liberals (a challenge shared with the Conservatives) but also challenges from breakaway socialists and minority nationalist groups. But the Party's ultimate share of the vote, and the seats in the House, justified Mr Wilson's calm

Below **22 February: Jimmy Reid,** Communist candidate for Central Dunbartonshire, campaigns. In spite of Reid's personal popularity in the area, the seat remained loyally Labour. Mr Reid nonetheless represented an important trend in the 1974 election — the success of minority interest candidates, nationalist or independent. Scottish Nationalists gained seven seats, Welsh Nationalists two. Independent Labour and Democratic Labour obtained one each

Below **8 February: Palestinian guerrillas** leave the Japanese embassy in Kuwait under police escort on their way to board a Japanese airliner to Aden. Five guerrillas took over the Japanese embassy and held 16 embassy officials, including the Ambassador, hostage. They demanded the release of four of their fellow terrorists who were hiding out on a hijacked ferry in Singapore after failing to blow up an offshore Shell oil installation. The four terrorists, members of the Japanese Red Army and the PFLP (Popular Front for the Liberation of Palestine), were brought to Kuwait from Singapore, and after the release of the hostages from the embassy all nine terrorists were allowed to leave the country

Associated Press

Press Association

Right **11 February: John Poulson** reflects after learning of his sentence of five years' imprisonment. Mr Poulson, 63-year-old former international architect, was charged with Mr William Pottinger, a senior Scottish Civil Servant, who received a like sentence. They were found guilty of one charge of conspiracy to corrupt and six charges of giving and receiving gifts as bribes

John Hillelson

Press Association

Above **28 February: A final,** election-day boost for the Liberal Party leader, Jeremy Thorpe. His return for his own constituency with an overwhelming majority was a personal triumph, and the Liberal Party's share of the vote (6,056,713) was a further step on the road to national recovery that had marked his leadership. Much resentment was felt by Liberals at the fact that they had polled nearly 20% of the national vote, and yet obtained only 2% of the available seats

Right **22 February: Pakistan's Prime Minister** Ali Bhutto exchanges a warm welcome with the Bangladesh Prime Minister Sheikh Mujibur Rahman after his announcement that Pakistan extended formal diplomatic recognition to Bangladesh. Mr Bhutto announced that he was acting in accordance with the 'unanimous opinion' of Muslim leaders gathered in Lahore for the Second Islamic Summit. India had been pressing Pakistan to recognise Bangladesh for some time, but Mr Bhutto had held out against it. He said that he felt he had now made the right decision for Pakistan although he was not personally happy about it

135

Popperfoto

Left **22 February: King Feisal of Saudi Arabia,** Guardian of the Holy Ground, photographed as he presided over the Second Islamic Summit

Below **22 February: King Feisal sits** crosslegged in Al Badshhi Mosque, Lahore, flanked on the left by Colonel Gaddafi of Libya and on the right by Sheikh Sabah of Kuwait. The service of the Second Islamic Summit opened with the prayer of the 29th of the month of Al Muharram Al Haram of the year 1394 of the Hegira

Above **21 February: The Busker King and Queen,** James Morris, 66, and Megan Aikman, 53, are crowned at the Buskers Festival organised by the London Tourist Board. Both of them earn their living by doing the rounds of theatre and cinema queues in the West End, singing for their supper

Rex Features

Gar

MARCH

Below **11 March: The Archbishop of Canterbury, Dr Michael Ramsey,** with his wife announces his retirement from Lambeth Palace. Dr Ramsey had long since decided to continue the custom of Church of England bishops by retiring at the allotted time of three score years and ten. His retirement took effect from 15 November 1974 – his 70th birthday. He was enthroned as the 100th occupant of the throne of St Augustine on 27 June 1961, and his 13-year term was marked by world-wide journeys to promote church unity. His, to some minds premature, retirement left a problem of succession as there was no one obvious in view to succeed him

Associated Press

Left **11 March: Dr Ramsey,** Archbishop of Canterbury, standing in the precincts of Canterbury Cathedral

Eve Arnold

Right **5 March: Harold Wilson returns** to 10 Downing Street as the new British Prime Minister of a minority government. This was the culmination of a five-day constitutional crisis following the February 28 General Election (see February, page 133). The election results left Wilson's Labour Party with the largest number of seats in the House of Commons (301), but with no overall majority. Prime Minister Edward Heath's Conservative Party followed only five seats behind with 296. But the balance was held by powerful minority holdings: 14 Liberal seats and 23 others, Ulster Unionists, Nationalists and Independent Labour members. Edward Heath did not immediately resign on hearing the results, but spent the weekend of the 2/3 March seeking an alliance with the Liberals and Ulstermen, which would have given him a workable majority. The proffered terms, however, did not suit Liberal Leader Jeremy Thorpe, and on the 4th Heath resigned and Wilson was asked by the Queen to form an administration

Below **25 March: Prince Philip** is overturned and kicked while pursuing his hobby of driving four-in-hand. The accident happened in Windsor Park when the wagonette he was driving overturned. No serious injury resulted

Popperfoto

Press Association

Right **7 March: Miss Marjorie Wallace**, 20, the American Miss World who won her title in November 1973 drives to London Airport after being deposed by the Mecca organisation. Miss Wallace flew home to the US after being stripped of her title for the unsavoury press coverage she had received. She was due back in England on 27 March to appear in Marylebone Court to give evidence against footballer George Best, a former boyfriend, who allegedly stole £6,000 worth of property from her flat. Her name was also linked with pop singer Tom Jones and millionaire racing driver Peter Revson

Press Association

Below **3 March: The mangled remains of a Turkish DC10** bear witness to the world's worst air disaster: 345 people were killed, including the crew of 11, when the plane crashed into the Forest of Ermenonville a few minutes after take-off from Orly Airport, Paris. There were no survivors. Eyewitnesses thought that the aircraft had exploded in flight only seconds before crashing and the fact that seven bodies were discovered nine miles from the scene of the crash supported this theory. The plane cut a mile-long swathe through the forest and debris was scattered over a vast area. The many rescue workers who arrived at the scene in record time soon realised that there was no rescue work to be done. They set about the gruesome task of gathering up human remains and putting them in plastic bags. Ghoulish sightseers had to be kept firmly in check by the police. It was thought that some 200 of the passengers were British who had been transferred to the DC10 flight because of an industrial dispute by some of Heathrow Airport's staff

Sygma/Andanson

Rex Features

Above **March: Bereaved relatives** of the victims of the Turkish DC10 air crash near Paris hold a funeral service at the site of the accident

Right **26 March: Denis Healey,** the Labour government's Chancellor of the Exchequer, makes the traditional gesture as he leaves 11 Downing Street to present his budget to the House of Commons. For a man who had previously undertaken to make the rich howl, he presented a moderate budget, a few mild yelps being all he provoked. But his position as the Chancellor of a minority government was not strong enough to carry the draconian proposals that some of his followers would have liked to see

Associated Press

Below **20 March: Police search** for clues along the Mall, London, scene of the attempted kidnapping of Princess Anne

Right **20 March: The kidnapper's** white Ford Escort is parked in front of Princess Anne's Daimler and broken glass marks the spot of the near-disaster. The Princess and her husband were driving back from an engagement when the Ford Escort slewed in front of their chauffeur-driven car and a man leapt out and fired a hail of bullets into the Daimler. The chauffeur, Alexander Callender, and the Personal Detective, Inspector James Beaton, were both injured, but Captain Phillips and Princess Anne were unhurt, although shaken by the incident. A uniformed policeman, PC Michael Hills, who was on duty nearby, rushed to the scene and was shot in the stomach. A journalist, Mr Brian McConnell, who was passing in a taxi, went to the defence of the Princess and was shot in the chest. Although all four of the injured received serious wounds their condition later was said to be satisfactory. A man, Ian Ball, 26, was arrested in connection with the shooting and charged with attempting to murder Princess Anne's bodyguard, James Wallace Beaton, who had received the most serious injuries
Associated Press

Associated Press

Above **26 March: Three Britons,** Carol Maystone, 21, Derek King, 24, expedition leader, and Peter Bird, 26, set off from Gibraltar on the first leg of their journey round the world. The three were to share equal rowing duties but were expecting help from the trade winds after they had worked their way down the African coast to take them across the Atlantic to Panama. They were hoping to be back in Gibraltar by the summer of 1976

Press Association

Left **7 March: Mr John Erlichman**, formerly one of President Nixon's closest aides and advisor on domestic affairs who resigned in connection with the Watergate affair, is indicted again. He and Mr Charles Colson, another of Mr Nixon's close associates, were charged with conspiracy to organise and carry out the burglary of the office of Dr Daniel Ellberg's psychiatrist in Los Angeles. Dr Ellsberg had leaked secret Pentagon papers to the Press, and the White House was looking for something with which to discredit him. So the White House 'plumbers' unit, Nixon's private security force, was formed. Mr Erlichman was also charged on four separate counts of making false declarations to the FBI and to grand juries

Camera Press

Press Association

14 March: A demo with a difference. Paris police face an unusual problem as demonstrating farmers, angry at the closing of a slaughterhouse, urge their bulls to charge the police. The confused and reluctant bulls milled about causing chaos and hilarity among the onlookers

Gamma/Jean-Claude Francolon

Left **10 March: The last act of the Second World War?** Although there may be more Japanese soldiers surviving in Pacific island fastnesses, at the time of this surrender, in a jungle clearing in the Philippines, Lieutenant Onada was the last soldier of the war to lay down his arms. He had gone to war more than 30 years before with a warning from his mother that he would be ostracised if he surrendered. His training also had led him to expect a prolonged spell out of contact with other units if the war should go badly. His 29 years in the jungle had been spent in surviving and collecting intelligence on the whereabouts of Philippine troops in case the Japanese army should come back. Although he had heard rumours of the Japanese surrender, he felt he could not personally give up without orders from his commander

Left **12 March: Looking extraordinarily fit** Hiroo Onada greets his parents on his return to Tokyo. He was given a hero's welcome by crowds of thousands

Below **26 March: Edward Kennedy senior** proudly escorts his son on a skiing trip. In 1973 Edward Kennedy junior had to have his right leg amputated because of cancer. To be skiing within a year of the operation was another amazing example of the Kennedy family determination to rise above any misfortune, however great

Press Association

143

Sygma/John Beard

Associated Press

Left **March 1974: Emperor Haile Selassie** of Ethiopia, effective ruler of the country since 1916, attends a ceremony to mark the battle of Adowa, a victory over the Italians. But the 81-year-old Emperor had battles of his own to fight during March, as civil unrest grew and his army became disaffected and mutinous

Right **1 March: A young officer** explains to his soldiers the need to mutiny and his objectives. The combined civil and military unrest forced the Emperor to make conciliatory Cabinet changes

Below **7 March: Demonstrators** and police clash in Addis Ababa. The drought of 1973 coupled with high inflation and rising prices led to strikes and demands for greater political freedom. On top of this, discontent in the armed forces was rife as soldiers demanded better pay and conditions

Gamma/Michel Laurent

Gamma/Michel Laurent

Below **24 March: General Idi Amin** speaks to the Organisation of African Unity shortly after the attempted military coup in Uganda. The abortive coup was led by Brigadier Charles Arube, the former Army Chief of Staff, who had recently returned from a military course in the Soviet Union. A military spokesman for President Amin said that when Arube learned that the coup had failed he shot himself twice and later died in hospital. Most of the soldiers responsible for the uprising belonged to the 2,000-strong Lugbara tribe which had been showing signs of increasing unrest since the body of Foreign Minister Michael Odonga, a Lugbara, was discovered floating in the Nile. President Amin was reported to have said that there had been a number killed in the up-rising but it was impossible to estimate how many. He added that those responsible for the shooting would be dealt with 'according to the laws of Uganda'

Associated Press

Gamma/Gian-Franco Gorgoni

Left **7 March: The view from the control tower** of the Paris Charles de Gaulle Airport which was inaugurated on the 7th by the French Prime Minister Pierre Messmer. The new airport, 15 miles north of Notre Dame, is expected to be dealing with 40 million passengers per year by 1980

Above **27 March: The scene outside** New York's Loew's Theatre on the night of the world première of *The Great Gatsby*, David Merrick's production based on Scott Fitzgerald's famous novel. The car used here for period flavour is a Rolls Royce—an echo of Gatsby's yellow-painted car that played such an important part in the plot

Below **14 March: A girl tends** two seriously injured soldiers while a third lies dead on the ground after being shot on the steps of St Mary's Roman Catholic Church, Belfast. The terrorist responsible for the killing escaped through the crowd of worshippers. Violence increased in Ulster throughout March and what was believed to be Belfast's biggest bomb – 500lb – exploded in a booby-trapped truck in Royal Avenue

Bottom **7 March: The shattered,** twisted façade of Belfast's former Grand Central Hotel, Royal Avenue, which now houses the First Regiment, Royal Horse Artillery. Miraculously, although 24 people were injured in the explosion, no one was killed

Popperfoto

Press Association

Camera Press

Above **18 March: Four policemen** unceremoniously hoist a student from Essex University into a waiting police van. Two hundred police moved in to break the picket on the University's campus at the request of the Vice-Chancellor Dr Albert Sloman. The students blocked the main road into the campus to prevent lorries bringing in food supplies and glass to repair £6,000 worth of damage to broken windows done in earlier riots; 105 students were arrested but Miss Rusty Davis, President of the Student's Union, said that other universities had promised reinforcements. The increasing militancy was due to disciplinary proceedings taken against 36 students during the previous term

Right **18 March: Not Guy Fawkes,** but Essex University's Vice-Chancellor is being burnt for his 'sins'. Essex University students condemned the use of police on the campus and blamed the Vice-Chancellor, Dr Sloman, for urging their intervention

Rex Features

Camera Press

Above **28 March**: **M Alain Colas** finishes his round-the-world voyage in his trimaran *Manureva* in a record time of 168 days. He clipped 57 days off the time of the late Sir Francis Chichester who made the single-handed voyage in 1966/7. M Alain Colas was greeted by his Tahitian fiancée, Tebura, as he sailed into St Malo harbour. He was several days overdue as a lack of wind and dense fog had held him up in the Bay of Biscay. The 30-year-old Frenchman was exhausted from seven sleepless days in the Bay while he kept watch to avoid collision with tankers and freighters. Of his feelings about the voyage he said 'I have seen many, many things about which I must now think. I will no longer be the same man again'

149

Right **14 March: Actress Mia Farrow** proudly presents her husband, André Previn, with a new addition to the family: a 6lb 14oz son, Fletcher Farrow Previn

Below **29 March: Alexander Solzhenitsyn,** the exiled Soviet writer, meets his wife and four children at Zurich Airport after over a month of anxious separation. Natalya, his 35-year-old wife, was able to bring his valuable files and manuscripts with her

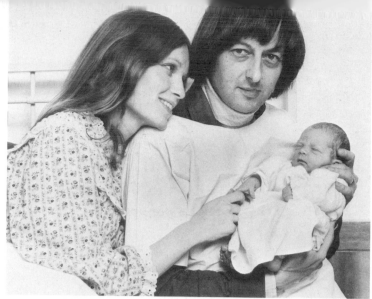

Camera Press

Associated Press

Rex Features

Rex Features

Above **16 March: Dr Marcello Caetano,** Portugal's Prime Minister. Some 200 troops were involved in an anti-government rising in which they staged a march on Lisbon. The troops were from the 5th Infantry Regiment, which was stationed at Caldas da Rainta, 28 miles north of Lisbon. They incarcerated their newly arrived commander, his second-in-command and other pro-government officers in the barracks and set off for Lisbon in armoured cars. They were led by officers, thought to belong to other regiments, who had infiltrated the barracks. Only eight miles outside Lisbon the insurgents came up against a strong force of military and police. After learning that there was no support for their cause in Lisbon the rebels returned to their barracks, closely followed by loyal soldiers who were quickly joined by reinforcements with tanks. The rebels capitulated later in the day, and some 20 officers of varying ranks were arrested

Right **24 March: Italian police** investigate one of the hideouts where Paul Getty jnr was held by his allegedly Mafiosa kidnappers shortly before the arrest of Girolamo Piromalli, said to be involved in the kidnapping and one of Calabria's Mafia

29 March: For the most energetic man in the world, marriage is something that happens between flights. Returning from Moscow and Europe, Henry Kissinger paused to marry Nancy Sharon Maginnes and to honeymoon briefly in Mexico, before boarding another plane for the Middle East

Sygma/Lee Romero

APRIL

2 April: Paris. Georges Pompidou, President of the French Republic for five years, dies. For months France had been rife with speculation about the President's health but nonetheless his death at the age of 62, came as a great shock to political circles in Paris. The political life of the Fifth Republic had been centred on the head of state for so long that concern was felt for the future

Left **A requiem mass** is held for the dead President at Notre Dame Cathedral

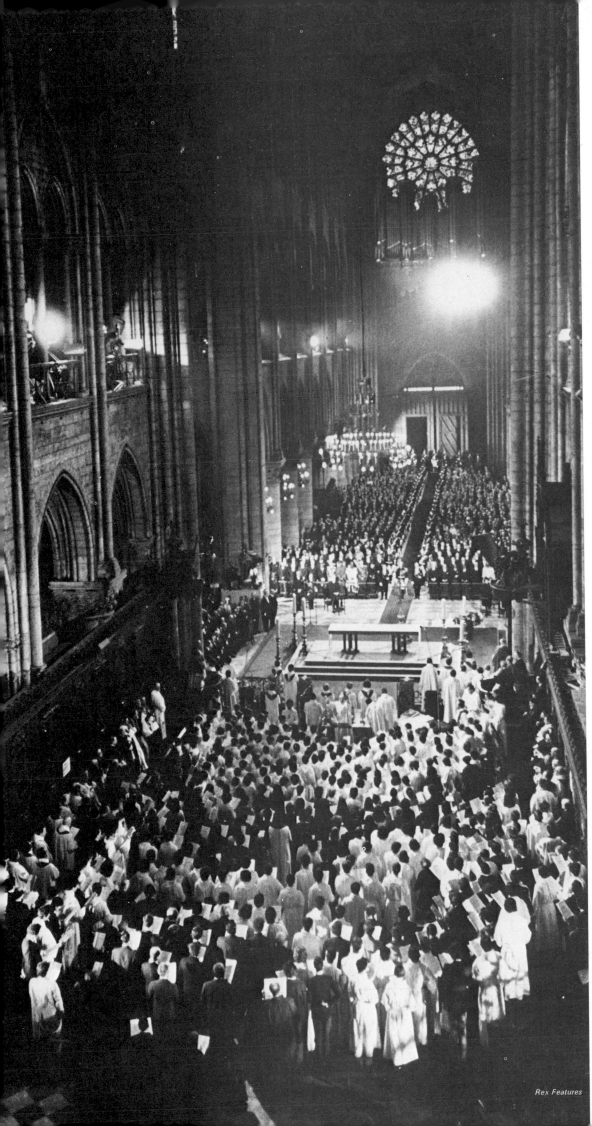

Rex Features

Sygma/Alain Noques

Above **2 April: Pompidou's widow** is escorted to her car after the funeral service

Below **At the President's own wish** his tricolour-draped coffin is buried in privacy at the tiny village of Orvilliers, 25 miles west of Paris

Rex Features

Right **14 April: The White Ensign** flies again over the Suez Canal as the Royal Navy co-operates with the US Navy and the Egyptian Navy in a massive drive to clear the Suez Canal of the detritus of war, and the blockships sunk during the 1956 Suez Crisis

Below **14 April: The Mexican yacht,** *Sayula II* nears the finishing line at Portsmouth, England, in the Whitbread round-the-world race, to win 40 hours ahead of the Royal Navy entry *Adventure*. The race had been extremely tough, with two crews losing a man overboard in the long haul through the roaring forties

Associated Press

Associated Press

Central Press

Left **6 April: The Oxford crew** show their Cambridge rivals a clean pair of heels during the annual Oxford and Cambridge boat race on London's tideway. Oxford won over the three-mile course by five lengths

Associated Press

2 April: The *QE 2* **drifts** powerless on the calm Atlantic after her crew and passengers had been evacuated to another ship. This latest incident in the *QE 2*'s troubled career happened when all three of her boilers broke down as the result of a fuel leak

Left **2 April: Launches shuttle** passengers from the giant *QE 2* to the smaller *Sea Venture*

Rex Features

Below **3 April: Wilbur Mills,** vice-chairman of the Congressional Committee on Internal Revenue, announces the committee's recommendation that President Nixon pay $476,431 outstanding income tax. Later the White House agreed to pay $432,787. The incident was a double blow to Mr Nixon. The financial blow was severe enough, but the committee's decision, with its implication that the President had avoided, or attempted to avoid, paying tax, lowered his nationwide popularity rating even more than the long list of Watergate revelations

Right **3 April: A copy** of part of the Nixon 1970 tax return

Associated Press

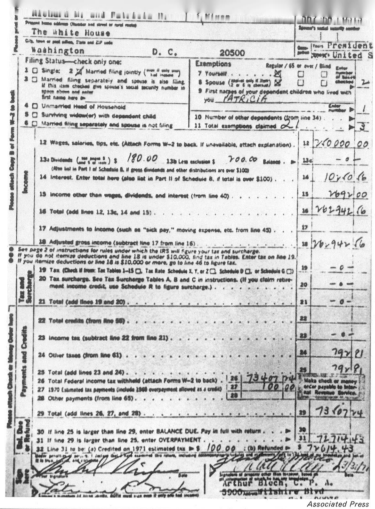

Associated Press

Right **3/4 April: Cincinnati, Ohio.** The awesome spout of a tornado touches down to embark on its career of destruction. In the worst onslaught of tornadoes for 49 years, 336 US citizens were killed in 11 midwestern states. Incalculable damage was done to property, water supplies, power supplies, and crops. President Nixon declared five states disaster areas

Popperfoto

Left **22 April: General Mullah Mustafa Barzani,** the 76-year-old leader of the Kurdish forces that revolted against Iraqi rule in April 1974. On the 22nd, Barzani's clandestine radio, the Voice of Kurdistan, announced the execution of 19 captured Iraqi officers in reprisal against the shooting of 11 prominent Kurdish figures the previous week. These incidents precipitated still more fighting between Iraqi and Kurdish forces. The disturbances arose from the Kurd's rejection of Iraq's proposals for their autonomy. The Kurdish demands included an independent Kurdish state, a share in the administration of the oil-rich Kirkuk region, and the establishment of Kurdish language schools

Below **April 1974: Kurdish tribesmen** look out from their dominating heights over the Alibey Pass, the scene on 1 April of a battle in which they routed a 3,000-strong Iraqi brigade

Rex Features

Sygma/C. Simonpietri

157

April saw continued fighting between North and South Vietnamese forces in South Vietnam. Battalion-sized encounters happened throughout the month, and, in spite of the continued presence of the International Control Commission (set up in 1973 after the Kissinger/Le Duc Tho negotiated ceasefire), the ceasefire agreement itself was as good as dead

Left **A government gun boat** patrols the Mekong Delta

Right **24 April: Government troops** clear the edges of a dirt road 30 miles north-west of Saigon

Below **3 April: Government** troops collect rations and help a bewildered civilian woman to safety during the communist attack on the Duc Hue Ranger Base

Rex Features

Rex Features

Rex Features

Far right **15 April: A girl,** believed to be the kidnapped heiress, Patricia Hearst, is pictured during a robbery at the Hibernian Bank, San Francisco. The robbery was conducted by the Symbionese Liberation Army, Patricia's kidnappers, and the participation of Miss Hearst lent strength to their claim that Miss Hearst had become converted to their point of view and had joined their movement. It was noticed, however, that the other bank robbers trained their guns on the girl as much as on the bank staff and many, including her parents, believed that Miss Hearst had been acting under duress throughout

Right **A photograph taken by** the Symbionese Liberation Army to support their claim that Miss Hearst had joined them. It was also released by the FBI as an identification picture when a warrant was issued for Miss Hearst's arrest as a material witness to bank robbery

Right **29 April: Metropolitan Anthony Bloom,** the senior Russian Orthodox prelate in Western Europe, resigns in a disagreement with the central authority of his church over the treatment of dissidents in Russia, in particular the case of Solzhenitsyn

Right **10 April: 'I am unable to carry the burden any longer.'** Israel's Premier, Mrs Golda Meir, announces her resignation after five years as Israel's leader. Although she denied that her resignation had anything to do with the power struggle over the status of Defence Minister Moshe Dayan (widely blamed for Israel's unreadiness in the Yom Kippur war), it was the struggle between pro- and anti-Dayanists that made it impossible for her to continue

Press Association

Popperfoto

Associated Press

Popperfoto

Rex Features

Sipa/Michel Crosby

Left **21 April: Senator Edward Kennedy** and his wife visit Moscow's tomb of the unknown soldier during the Senator's week-long fact-finding visit to the USSR. Less decorous scenes were enacted when Kennedy asked Moscow University students whether they wanted their country to spend more or less on defence. A professor shouted that the Senator's question was a provocation. The remark was not translated. Other remarks by Kennedy on immigration were not translated to the audience, and eventually the interpreter took it upon himself to declare that Kennedy was not feeling well and the meeting would have to end. In spite of Kennedy's insistence that he was all right, the meeting was declared closed

Above **22 April: The Kennedy's** go sightseeing in the Kremlin

Associated Press   *Press Association*

Top left **21 April: Ronald Milhench** is charged with criminal deception in trying to obtain £25,000 from Associated Newspapers Ltd. Mr Milhench was at the centre of the 'land deals' affair and the forging of Mr Harold Wilson's name at the bottom of a letter relating to land in Cheshire

Top right **Kathleen Milhench** pictured a few months before her death

Right **21 April: Police search** Chasewater Lake, Staffordshire, during an extension of their enquiry into the background of Ronald Milhench. Milhench's wife, Kathleen, was killed when a car, driven by Milhench, plunged into the lake

Right **18 April: Janie Jones** is sentenced to seven years' imprisonment for controlling prostitutes. She was cleared of 11 charges of blackmail. In his remarks the judge called Miss Jones 'evil', and made it clear that he believed her to have used blackmail as part of her prostitution service. The trial, which lasted three months, had heard evidence of how Miss Jones persuaded girls to go to bed with men in the hope of getting work on television or in films. Later the threat of disclosing their behaviour was used to persuade them to continue in prostitution

Rex Features   *Press Association*

Popperfoto

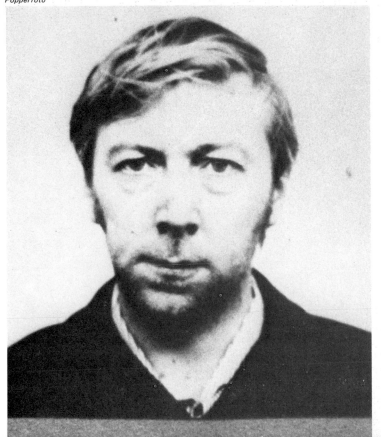

Popperfoto

Left **13 April: Kenneth Lennon,** whose body was found murdered in a ditch in Surrey, pictured some months before his death. Three days before he died he left a 17-page statement with the Council for Civil Liberties claiming that the British Special Branch had co-opted him into being an informant for them on the IRA. Special Branch, he alleged, had 'arranged' to clear him of various charges if he co-operated in infiltrating the IRA community in Luton, Bedfordshire. His role was detected by the IRA, and his murder was believed to have been an IRA execution

Above **18 April: Hamburg. A West German policeman** shoots a bank robber at point-blank range as he emerges from the bank holding his hostage. The robber (partially obscured by the hostage) had already killed one policeman and wounded another. The incongruous figure in the foreground is a police officer — dressed, at the gunman's demand, in bathing trunks — who was to have driven his getaway car

25 April: Portugal. At dawn on the 25th Portuguese army units carried out a coup that displaced Dr Caetano, and exiled him and his ministers. Caetano's surrender was accepted by General Spinola, dismissed from the army only a month before for publishing a controversial book about Portugal's role in Africa.

The almost bloodless coup set up a seven-man junta, including Spinola, which promised to restore human rights to all Portuguese citizens and to hold early elections

Right **25 April: General Spinola,** leader of the Portuguese coup, pictured in Lisbon after he had accepted Dr Caetano's surrender

Bottom right **25 April: Civilians** distribute flowers to the liberating troops

Far right **1 May: Crowds celebrate May Day** just six days after the coup. The new régime was anxious to avoid any disturbances and had issued stern warnings to the extreme left groups. In the event all passed off peacefully

Rex Features

Gamma/Jean-Claude Francolon

Sygma/Henri Bureau

Top **25 April: Troops round** up former secret police agents. In many cases the soldiers had to step in to prevent crowds lynching ex-members of the DGS, Caetano's hated state police

Above **25 April: Crowds swarm** into the streets to welcome the coup

Rex Features

John Hillelson

Right **28 April: Syrian soldiers** celebrate the recapture of a hillside near Mount Hermon in the clashes that continued for weeks as the Syrians tried to take back the mountain, captured by the Israelis at the end of the October war.

Below **28 April: An Israeli** artillery piece moves up near Mount Hermon as the fighting spread to the whole Golan front

Associated Press

Associated Press

Left **April 1974: A thrice lucky girl** is 24-year-old Paloma Picasso. Heiress to Pablo Picasso's fortune, a film star in the film *Immoral Tales*, and designer of the jewellery she is here modelling

Sygma/Giancarlo Botti

Below: **21 April: All in the line of duty.** A London policeman puts his helmet to an unusual purpose as streaker, Michael O'Brien, removed his clothes and ran across the pitch at Twickenham where France were playing England in a rugby match. A determined match official runs up with a raincoat. The cause of their concern? Watching from the royal box was Princess Alexandra. So far 'no comment' from the royal party

Syndication International

Right **14 April: Joginder Singh** and David Doig celebrate their win in the East African Safari Rally. The 3,000-mile rally is considered the toughest in the world

Below **25 April: Seen together** in perhaps their most famous screen roles, as Antony and Cleopatra, are Richard Burton and Elizabeth Taylor, whose 10-year marriage ended as divorce proceedings began on the 25th. The Burton's marriage had suffered a number of ups and downs in previous months. The proceedings referred to 'irreconcilable differences'

Rex Features

Associated Press

Rex Features

1 May: On the streets and on balconies the people of Lisbon flocked out on May Day to celebrate their new-found freedom. In spite of government misgivings the demonstrations were orderly, with the atmosphere more of a carnival than of a political demonstration. (For other pictures see April, pages 164 and 165)

Rex Features

Below **1 May: A copy of the letter** from Nixon to General Haig ordering him not to answer questions put to him by the Senate Watergate Committee. The General refused to answer more than 100 questions, many of them relating to the donation of $100,000 to the President's election campaign by recluse millionaire, Howard Hughes

Below **1 May: A bulky best seller** is carried away by Ellen Miller, one of the first buyers at the Government Printing Office in Washington, when the transcripts of the White House Tapes were put on sale

Right **1 May: More buyers queue up** for their copy of the tape transcripts

May 1, 1974

Dear General Haig,

I am informed that you have been subpoenaed to testify before the Senate Select Committee on Presidential Campaign Activities on May 2, 1974.

It would be wholly inappropriate for the Committee to examine you about your activities as Chief of Staff or about information that has come to you in that position since your assumption of your present duties in May, 1973, or in your earlier position as a member of the staff of the National Security Council.

A President's Chief of Staff is inevitably very close to the President and functions as the President's right arm. He is often the means by which the President communicates with his lawyers on matters that are within the attorney-client privilege. It is also the means by which the President communicates with other members of the Executive Branch.

In your former capacity as a senior member of the National Security Council staff, you dealt with the most sensitive categories of information relating to the national security.

Whatever differences there are about the reaches of executive privilege generally, I am confident that the members of the Senate Select Committee will recognize that it is essential to any President that he be able to talk with complete freedom and candor with the person that occupies such a close relationship with him and who works so closely with him on the full range of executive functions.

While I have made every effort to waive privilege for former and present members of my staff to testify before the Senate Select Committee, I must regretfully decline in your case.

You are, therefore, directed not to testify about any information received or activities undertaken while you served as my Chief of Staff or as a member of the National Security Council staff.

Sincerely,

Richard Nixon

General Alexander M. Haig, Jr. (USA-Ret.)
Assistant to the President
The White House
Washington, D. C.

Popperfoto

Associated Press

Sygma/J. P. Laffont

Associated Press

Sygma/J. P. Laffont

Left **1 May: A smiling President Nixon** displays a scroll, bearing the names and comments of thousands of his supporters, presented to him by Mrs Francis Finnen of Malibu, California (*right*)

Above **13 May: The first sitting** of the House Judiciary Committee, to look into 'Watergate related' aspects of the administration, opens

May 1974: **Three events** from the Olympics of the Absurd held in California at Los Angeles by a group of young Americans trying to beat some of the records mentioned in the *Guinness Book of Records*. Handstands, goldfish swallowing and mass cigarette smoking, 110 at a time, were just three of the items which also included beer drinking, bubble-gum blowing and spaghetti eating

Sygma/Tony Korody

Sygma/Tony Korody

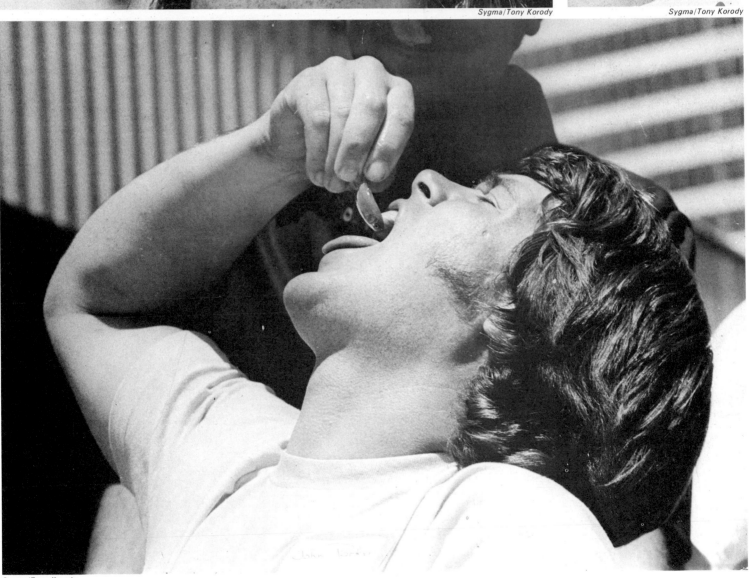

Sygma/Tony Korody

Rex Features

Right **7 May: Left-wing demonstrators** march through the streets of Calcutta to celebrate the rail strike paralysing the city. Attempts to extend the strike to a national level were foiled by massive arrests of railway workers, numbering more than 10,000 by the end of the month

Below **13 May: Thousands** pack on to the few trains leaving Delhi station as strikers are rounded up by police

Associated Press

Associated Press

Above **18 May: A sinister mound** appears in an unspecified part of India's dusty landscape as India conducted her first atomic test. The fears aroused all over the world by yet another entrant to the nuclear club were only slightly allayed by India's assurance that all atomic development in the country would be for peaceful purposes only

Sygma/Nik Wheeler

Far left **31 May**: **Geneva. Syria and Israel** agree on the details of a disengagement in the Golan Heights as the Finnish General in charge of the UN peacekeeping forces, General Silasvuo, reads the draft agreement. This agreement was seen as the outcome of months of negotiations by the US Secretary of State Henry Kissinger

Left **31 May**: **No longer on duty**, this Israeli gun crew on the Golan Heights can stand down

Below **May**: **Members of the British nursing profession** congregate in London for a rally to draw attention to their claims for higher basic pay. More and more nurses were leaving the country for higher-paying work abroad or turning to agency work, where less qualified nurses could earn £40 in a 40-hour working week. Towards the end of June 1974 it looked as though the nurses would succeed in getting an interim pay award before it could be decided whether or not their claims for higher basic pay could be fully met

Associated Press

Associated Press

May 1974: Ulster Protestants organise province-wide strike. On 12 May Ulster's Protestant workers launched a strike aimed to bring down the Ulster Executive set up by the Sunningdale agreement. The strike received the support of a large majority of Northern Irish people and was instantly effective. Within a fortnight it had brought the province to a halt without any essential services, power or food deliveries. The strike was enforced thoroughly and with a degree of coercion remarkable even in Ulster. In Larne, Co Antrim, club-swinging Protestant trusties patrolled the streets compelling businesses and shops to close

Press Association

Below: **27 May: Communal street-corner cooking** for Belfast families as the last of Ulster's gas and electricity supplies were cut off

Associated Press

Below **May 1974: Stormont is** besieged by protesting loyalists

Associated Press

Top **27 May: British soldiers** man a petrol station in an attempt to keep up the flow of at least minimum services

Above **15 May: British troops** guard food supplies as the strike called by Ulster's Protestants gripped the province and brought it to a standstill

Magnum/Gilles Peress

Above **28 May: Jubilant** Protestant demonstrations mark the fall of Brian Faulkner

Right **28 May: Brian Faulkner,** chief minister in the Northern Ireland Executive, resigns. The two-week strike had achieved its objective and brought the Executive to its knees

Rex Features

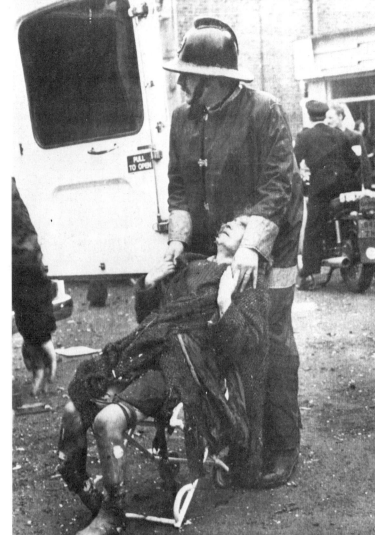

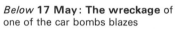

17 May: Horror comes to the South. For so long mercifully spared her sister city's troubles, Dublin was blitzed on the 17th by three car bombs which killed 27 and injured hundreds. A fourth bomb went off in Monaghan. Ulster extremist groups were naturally suspected, but none claimed responsibility

Right **17 May: The victim of terrorism**. An old lady, terribly injured, is wheeled into an ambulance

Below **17 May: The wreckage** of one of the car bombs blazes

Magnum/Gilles Peress

Press Association

Magnum/Gilles Peress

Popperfoto

Below **6 May: A dejected Willy Brandt** announces his resignation as West German Chancellor following a scandal that revealed that his personal assistant, Herr Guillaume, was a spy for East Germany

Associated Press

Associated Press

Top right **11 November 1972: As Willy Brandt** campaigns for the 1972 elections, Herr Guillaume (left, with crew-cut and glasses) listens. In May 1974 Guillaume's spying brought an end to Brandt's political career

Above **16 May: Helmut Schmidt,** Brandt's successor as Chancellor

Right **1 June: New President and new Chancellor** confer. Giscard d'Estaing and Herr Schmidt give a press conference after their Paris talks on the future of the EEC

Sygma/Henri Bureau

Associated Press

Rex Features

Rex Features

Left **27 May: The newly elected President of France,** M Valery Giscard d'Estaing, waves to the crowds on his way to the official investiture. He was elected in the final stage of the Presidential election on 19 May by a 1% margin over his nearest rival, Francois Mitterand

Sygma/Henri Bureau

Above **May 1974: François Mitterand,** the left-wing coalition leader, addresses supporters during his campaign. His impressive share of the total vote was the largest left-wing share of the suffrage since 1945

Rex Features

Above **A poster supporting Jaques Chaban Delmas,** the Gaullist candidate who dropped out during the first round of the election, is defaced by a sticker reflecting the general public unease at Delmas' history of tax avoidance. Fears that Gaullist supporters would abstain in the final election proved unfounded

Left **May 1974: Often accused of aloofness,** d'Estaing softens his image by joining in a game of football

Associated Press

Right **14 May: Dr Coggan, the Archbishop of York**, smiles for the Press at a conference announcing his appointment to the Archbishopric of Canterbury in succession to Dr Ramsey. Coggan, regarded as something of a conservative by younger bishops, took only four days to decide to accept the post

Associated Press

Above **28 May: The barely recognisable bodies** of demonstrators lie in the square of Brescia, Italy, after a bomb had exploded at an anti-Fascist rally, killing six and wounding 79

Right **7 May: Not the sentiments of the management**. Pro-divorce demonstrators in Italy painted this NO (to the proposed repeal of the Italian divorce laws) on Florence's famous Santa Maria basilica. The Italian electorate voted overwhelmingly to retain their divorce laws in spite of the stern opposition of the Church

Associated Press

Rex Features

Left **16 May: General Spinola**, the leader of the coup that toppled Caetano in Portugal, is elected the twelfth President of Portugal since it became a republic in 1910. Anxious to form a broad-based administration that would command popular support, Spinola included two Communists in his first Cabinet. Here the newly elected President is congratulated by representatives of the Roman Catholic Church — a body un-ashamedly relieved at Spinola's successful coup, for while it remains a powerful conservative force in Portugal itself, in the world at large its representatives have been among the most bitter critics of Portuguese rule in Africa

Popperfoto

Above **20 May: The Guru Maharaj Ji**, 16-year-old spiritual wonder, places the ring on his bride's finger at his marriage to 24-year-old Marolyn Lois Johnson in California

Associated Press

Left **May: Archbishop Makarios**, (*right*) President of Cyprus, is welcomed to Peking by China's leader, Chairman Mao Tse-tung

179

15 May: What makes them do it? The four apparently happy and healthy young men who, on 15 May, stormed and held the Israeli school at Maalot near the Lebanese border. Threatening to kill the 90 schoolchildren unless their demands were met, they demanded the release of 26 Arab prisoners in Israel and the Japanese responsible for the Lod Massacre. The Israeli government agreed to these demands but the deal broke down when the Arabs failed to get the necessary codeword from Damascus. Israeli troops had surrounded the building, and as the failure of the agreement became known they stormed the school in an attempt to kill the terrorists. The Arabs fired at the troops and threw hand-grenades among the children, killing 16 and wounding nearly all of them. One Arab killed himself, a second was killed by his own explosives, and a third was killed by the troops

Rex Features

Sygma/Richard Melloul

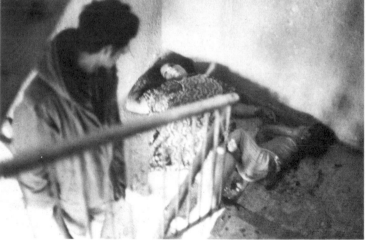

Rex Features

Above left **15 May: Israeli soldiers** wait to storm the school at Maalot in an attempt to save the children held hostage inside

Above right **15 May: A mother and child** killed as the terrorists stormed the school

Right **15 May: Soldiers** and civilians carry away the wounded

Rex Features

Sygma/Nik Wheeler

Popperfoto

Above **16 May: An Israeli** bomb explodes on a Lebanese village in reprisal for the Maalot massacre

Left **16 May: The remains of the refugee settlement** of Ain Helweh near Saida after the Israeli bombing. Twenty-seven were killed as aircraft struck at several camps in the Lebanon

Rex Features

Right **19 May**: **Timothy Davey** is reunited with his family after his release from prison in Turkey under a general amnesty declared by the Turkish parliament. Within 24 hours Davey was in trouble with the Turkish authorities again when he made unflattering references to the Turkish police and press. Davey's original offence had been the possession and sale of 60lb of hashish, for which he got a six-year jail sentence in 1971

Right **29 May**: **Pop superstar** David Cassidy takes a break during his London tour. At his concert at London's White City Stadium a 14-year-old girl was crushed in a crowd of Cassidy fans and subsequently died

Below **16 May**: **Chevening Place**, the magnificent 18th-Century house in which, it was announced on the 16th, Prince Charles would live. It was bequeathed to the nation by Lord Stanhope with just such a plan in mind. Chevening is near Sevenoaks in Kent

Press Association   *Associated Press*

Popperfoto

Right **24 May**: **A peeress in the supermarket.** Marcia Williams, Harold Wilson's private and sometimes controversial secretary, pictured shopping after the news that she had been awarded a life peerage

Associated Press

Associated Press

Left **May 1974: British actor** Roger Moore seen on location in Thailand with his co-star, Britt Ekland, during the making of the next Bond film, *The Man With the Golden Gun*

Above **May 1974: Tomas Moreno**, an apprentice matador, learns his trade the hard way. A mistimed pass with his cape led to his involuntary flight across the bullring. He was unhurt

Popperfoto

Right **3 May: Model Angie Berry** admires her ample proportions as rendered by sculptor James Butler for the Royal Academy's Summer exhibition in London. The price to have the larger-than-life Miss Berry in your own home? £2,500

Sygma/Rene Maestri

Above **26 May: Ronnie Peterson** wins the Monte Carlo Grand Prix

Right **17 May: Joe Mercer, temporary manager of England's football team** after the dismissal of Sir Alf Ramsay, talks to Martin Peters (*left*) and centre-forward Frank Worthington (*right*)

Left **15 May. France: An unknown gunman** covers himself with seven-year-old Xavier Lacheteau as he makes his getaway. Xavier and his mother were two of eight hostages taken by the gunmen after they had robbed a bank in Champigny-sur-Marne. The gunmen escaped with Xavier and his mother

Popperfoto

Press Association

JUNE

Left **2 June: China offers** to present two young giant pandas to London Zoo as a gift to Britain. It was thought that the gift would be of one male and one female panda. Edward Heath, leader of the Opposition, announced the news on his arrival in Hong Kong after his visit to China had ended

Associated Press

Above **4 June: Mrs Golda Meir** toasts her successor to the premiership of Israel, Yitzhak Rabin, before leaving her Jerusalem office. Mrs Meir, 76, said that she was tired from all the strain of the past months and that she had wanted to retire for the past year. In the summer of 1973 she was persuaded against retiring and she led the Labour Party into the October elections. The Yom Kippur war and six months of political unease followed. But despite the loss of her popularity in the poll ratings she always retained the regard of her countrymen. She was satisfied to have headed the caretaker government, and taken part in the negotiations with Dr Henry Kissinger that led to the disengagement with Syria, and thus to have ended her 25-year career in the Knesset with a success

Rex Features

Left **1 June: Part of the wreckage** caused by a devastating explosion which shattered the Nypro factory at Flixborough in the North of England. The explosion and resulting fire spread destruction over 100 acres, and Flixborough was declared a disaster area and evacuated. The explosion, the largest in England since WW II, occurred at the weekend and the loss of life, 29 dead, was comparatively small. Nypro was a specialist company formed to produce Caprolactam, essential for use in man-made fibres. The chemicals necessary for production were highly toxic and inflammable and it was thought that a leak might have developed in the piping, releasing a quantity of inflammable gas which exploded

Below **1 June: Rescue workers** help one of the 40 wounded away from the scene of disaster at the Flixborough Nypro factory

Rex Features

Rex Features

Left **11 June: Paris. Jean-Jacques Servan-Schreiber** gives a press conference. On the 9th he was dismissed from his post in the French cabinet for his opposition to the continuance of the French atmospheric nuclear tests. He had been in office only 11 days, and the speed of his dismissal was seen as a sign of President Giscard d'Estaing's determination to brook no challenge to his authority

Right **2 June: King Jigme Singye Wangchuk** is enthroned as the fourth hereditary ruler — Druk Gyalpo, the Dragon King — of the Himalayan Kingdom of Bhutan. In May 1974 an alleged plot to assassinate the 18-year-old monarch was uncovered and it was noted that the ceremony of tasting the rice wine as a precaution against poison was industriously performed. The ceremony took place in the Tashichhodzong, the stone and wooden fortress, presiding over the capital of Thimphu. On the auspicious hour of the serpent, 9 am, the King was clothed in the scarf of five colours by the Jey Kehmpo, the head Lama. The young King decided against a formal coronation with the raven's head crown, which was not an essential component of a Bhutanese coronation. Present at the ceremony were the Presidents of India and Pakistan and the Chogyal of Sikkim

Associated Press

Associated Press

Below **7 June**: **Lusaka, Zambia.** Frelimo's President Samora Machel (facing camera) embraces Major de Carvalho, the delegate of the Portuguese armed forces at the conference arranged with Frelimo about the future of Mozambique. Although the new Portuguese regime favoured eventual independence for the overseas possessions, Frelimo could not agree with the Portuguese as to how and when independence should take place. The talks broke down

Associated Press

Left **14 June**: **Miss Marjorie Wallace,** 20, the 1973 Miss World who was stripped of her title, is seen leaving the Methodist Hospital in Indianapolis where she was kept for 10 days after taking an overdose of drugs. With the ex-Miss World are her mother and Mr Bob Sucko, Director of Public Information for the hospital

Right **8 June**: **London. Another martyr for old Ireland,** and a sight that shocked many Londoners. IRA members march through the streets in semi-military style bearing the coffin of Michael Gaughan, who died on hunger strike in Parkhurst prison on 3 June. There was widespread feeling that a uniformed procession on this scale was provocative, and possibly illegal

Popperfoto   *Rex Features*

14 June: **Belfast. A British soldier** lies on the ground (*right*) wounded by the debris from a bomb detonated outside the BBC headquarters in Belfast. The Provisional IRA had long regarded the BBC as little more than a British government propaganda agency, and had been bitterly critical of its news coverage in Ulster. After the explosion a spokesman for the BBC said that nothing would deter the BBC from its policy of impartial reporting

Associated Press

Press Association

Above **7 June: The mother and sister** (*right and far right*) of Dolours and Marion Price sit at a press conference in King's Cross, London, protesting against the force-feeding of hunger strikers. With them are the father and wife of Gerald Kelly, also on hunger strike, and the mother of Hugh Feeney, another hunger striker. The Price sisters gave up their hunger strike after an agreement had been reached with the Home Secretary, Mr Roy Jenkins. It was thought that pressure had been brought to bear by the kidnappers of Lord and Lady Donoughmore. The end of the Price sisters' hunger strike brought about the release of the Donoughmores

Right **9 June: The Earl and Countess** of Donoughmore photographed in Dublin Police HQ after their release by the kidnappers in Phoenix Park, Dublin. Lord and Lady Donoughmore were kidnapped after driving to their home near Clonmel from a dinner party. Lord Donoughmore was hit on the head five times by a pistol and his wife was struck once. They were blindfolded, bundled into a car and driven at high speeds through twisting country lanes. They were transferred into other cars twice and then taken to a bungalow. They were kept there for nearly a week but were well treated by their captors, whom they described as being 'very humane' and 'courteous'. They were fed and their wounds were carefully treated. Lord Donoughmore said that he thought the kidnappers might have been Provisional IRA and police believed that they might have been the same gang responsible for the £6m art theft from the home of Sir Alfred Beit. The Donoughmores were told by their captors that they would be released within 24 hours after the Price sisters and other hunger strikers had abandoned their fast. No ransom note was sent. At 12.30 am on the day of their release the Donoughmores were woken up and told: 'You are in luck. The hunger strikers have given up.' They were then blindfolded and taken to a car and, after a long drive, released. The kidnappers managed to get through a road-block just before the Donoughmores were released. As luck would have it for the kidnappers, the police waved their car through without making an identity check

Popperfoto

Keystone

Bipna

Right **14 June:** **The most evocative trapping of a military funeral,** the riderless charger, is led from Windsor Castle to precede the coffin of its master, the Duke of Gloucester. The Duke, who died on 10 June, was the last of Queen Elizabeth's uncles to die. As a young man his ambition had been a military career, but his closeness to the throne after the abdication of his brother brought this to an end. During the illness of George VI he was a potential regent of Great Britain until his niece came of age in 1947

Below **14 June:** **Marching behind the coffin,** as it passed through Windsor on the way to the family cemetery at Frogmore, were the Duke of Edinburgh, Prince Richard of Gloucester, Prince Charles and (*behind*) the Duke of Kent

Right **14 June:** **The coffin is carried away** from the altar of St George's Chapel, Windsor, at the end of the Duke of Gloucester's funeral service. Behind walk his widow, his son and daughter-in-law, the Queen, Prince Philip and other members of the Royal Family

Keystone

Gamma/J. P. Bonnotte

Left **16 June: A smile of confidence** from Queen Elizabeth as she watches her filly, Highclere, in the saddling enclosure at Chantilly before the Prix de Diane. Highclere won the mile and two-and-a-quarter-furlong race by two lengths, bringing the Queen the largest racing prize she had yet won, and her first win in this classic French race

Right **20 June: Linda Lovelace,** star of the controversial sex film, *Deep Throat*, catches the eye at Royal Ascot when she arrived, wearing a man's morning suit, minus the shirt, showing a deep throat all of her own. Punters were laying odds on her form with almost the alacrity they were placing money on the horses

UPI

Associated Press

Above **6 June: William Craig,** Glen Barr, Ian Paisley and Harry West smile from the platform of a political rally in Northern Ireland organised to celebrate the Protestant faction's successful stand against the Sunningdale agreement and power sharing (see May, page 174)

Left **June 1974: Smoke billows** from the ornate Edwardiana of Southsea's South Parade Pier after fire had broken out during location filming for Ken Russell's rock musical, *Tommy*. Two hundred people escaped from the building, among them Oliver Reed, starring in the production

Associated Press

Below **7 June: From the despatch box to the baton.** Ex-prime minister Edward Heath consoles himself out of office by taking the baton from André Previn to conduct the London Symphony Orchestra. Heath's love of music is almost as well known as his enthusiasm for yachting, and André Previn spoke warmly of the support he had given music throughout his political career

Rex Features

Rex Features

12–18 June: President Nixon's Middle East pilgrimage. During a hectic week, President Nixon visited Egypt, Syria, Saudi Arabia, Israel and Jordan. Shaking the dust of Watergate from his heels, the President braved the dust and sand of the desert as he visited the pyramids, and drove through Cairo to what was little short of a hero's welcome. But solid achievement showed through the flurry of diplomatic hyperbole — a two-way economic pact with Egypt to supply nuclear reactors and fuel for Egypt in exchange for joint development of her oil stocks

Associated Press

NIXON'S MIDEAST ITINERARY

- Damascus
- JUNE 16·17 ISRAEL
- JUNE 15·16 SYRIA
- Tel Aviv
- Amman
- Mediterranean Sea
- Jerusalem
- Suez Canal
- Cairo
- JUNE 17·18 JORDAN
- SINAI PENINSULA
- Gulf of Suez
- Gulf of Aqaba
- JUNE 12·14 EGYPT
- JUNE 14·15 SAUDI ARABIA
- 0 100 Miles
- Red Sea

Above **Nixon's** Middle East itinerary

Top **Not the first westerner** to look good in Arab dress. A montage from an Egyptian magazine shows Nixon in a *Kaffish*, the traditional Arab headdress

Left **14 June: The Russian ballet dancers,** Valery and Galina Panov, arrive in Vienna after the successful outcome of their two-year struggle to be allowed to emigrate from the USSR to Israel. In 1972 they were dismissed from the Kirov Ballet for applying to go to Israel

Rex Features

Rex Features

Above **12 June: A tumultuous welcome** for Nixon as an open motorcade takes him through Cairo

Left **12 June: Business and pleasure.** Nixon and Sadat shake hands as if clinching a deal in front of Egypt's most famous spectacle – the Pyramids

Below **14 June: King Feisal greets Nixon** as his plane arrives in Jeddah, Saudi Arabia. At a banquet given that evening Feisal told the President that a lasting peace in the Middle East was impossible until Isreal had satisfied all the Arab demands, including the return of Jerusalem and all the occupied territory, and self-determination for the Palestinian people

Popperfoto

15 June: London, Red Lion Square. Police and left-wing demonstrators clashed as a protest march, organised by a group called 'Liberation', tried to break up a meeting of the right-ring National Front

Below **15 June: The cause of the trouble.** The National Front march is cordoned off by the police to prevent clashes with the rival demonstration

Left **15 June: Violence erupts** as the left-wing demonstrators try to force the police cordon. In the centre of the crowd, facing the camera, is Kevin Gately, who later died of a brain haemorrhage caused by a blow to the head. The demonstration organisers complained of police brutality, but other bystanders spoke of a deliberate attack on the police by part of the left-wing demonstration. A police inspector who had been at the demonstration also died, possibly as a result of injuries received

Press Association

Press Association

Magnum/Ian Berry

Right **11 June: London. William Whitelaw** is appointed Chairman of the Conservative Party in succession to Lord Carrington. This placed on his adequately broad back the responsibility of re-shaping the Conservative image for the next election (which Labour Prime Minister Harold Wilson might have announced at any time) in an attempt to win back the voters who had defected to the Liberals in the February election

Left **22 June: A huge demonstration,** headed by a solitary banner, makes its way along the Thames Embankment, London, in silent protest against the death of Kevin Gately in the Red Lion Square riot a week before. Gately died after alleged police brutality in the rioting which broke out during a demonstration by both the extreme right and the extreme left in Red Lion Square on 15 June

Press Association

Popperfoto

Above **25 June: Dr Rose Dugdale,** 33, Oxford graduate daughter of a millionaire stock-broker, and self-styled 'Freedom Fighter for Ireland', is sentenced to nine years' imprisonment for receiving 19 stolen paintings worth over £6m. The paintings were stolen from the Co Wicklow home of Sir Alfred and Lady Beit in April 1974. A group of three men and a woman broke into Russborough House, held up Sir Alfred and Lady Beit and tore the paintings out of their frames. A ransom note demanding £500,000 was sent to the director of the National Gallery in Dublin. Later Dr Dugdale was found by police in possession of the paintings in Co Cork. When asked by the court if she wanted to make a statement or give evidence, Dr Dugdale made a passionate revolutionary speech about the English oppression of Ireland. Much of the speech was incoherent and Dr Dugdale appeared to be under great stress. Earlier in the hearing her solicitor. Mr Myles Shevlin, left the court after asking to be relieved of her defence. Charges alleging that Dr Dugdale took part in the armed robbery of the paintings were dropped

24 June: A harpoon gun is aimed at the Japanese delegation of the International Whaling Commission as it arrives at Riverbank House, London. Members of the *Friends of the Earth* environmentalist pressure group had brought the harpoon with them as part of a protest to persuade delegates to vote for a 10-year moratorium on whale hunting. The Japanese, together with the Russians, are largely responsible for the vast annual slaughter of whales

UPI

Right **17 June: Anarchy and affluence meet**. The driver of an expensive Rolls-Royce convertible watches as flames belch from Westminster Hall. At 8.22 am the London Press Association received a message to say that a bomb had been planted in the Houses of Parliament. In only six minutes the area was cleared and, as the bomb exploded, 11 people were injured. A gas main was fractured, starting fierce fires. The attack was seen as the most serious breach of security precautions that the IRA had yet achieved in London

17 June: Here a fireman fights to save the 14th-century Westminster Hall, damaged as fire spread from the neighbouring canteen where the bomb had been planted. In the background Big Ben records the fact that the fire had been burning for almost an hour and a half

Right **5 June**: **Derby Day at Epsom** and Snow Knight, the 66–1 outsider, leads the field home; behind him is Imperial Prince, another outsider, at 20–1, and, leading the bunched group, the second favourite Giacometti, 5–2, who came in third. Snow Knight was owned by Mr Neil Phillips, a Canadian tax lawyer, and trained by British trainer Mr Peter Nelson. Although the bookmakers cleaned up, with most of the 250,000 punters at Epsom putting their money on the French horse, Nonoalco, or on Giacometti, Mr Phillips made a handsome profit on top of his £89, 229 prize money with a £100 each way bet. The Queen, accompanied by Prince Philip, the Queen Mother and Princess Alexandra and her husband, watched the race

Keystone   *Associated Press*

Rex Features

Left **27 June: President Valéry Giscard d'Estaing** (*centre*) entertains the Shah of Iran and his Empress, Farah, in style at Versailles Palace. Seated on the Shah's right is Mme Giscard d'Estaing and on the Empress's left is the French Premier, M Jacques Chirac. In the course of the Shah's official visit to France, the foreign ministers of both countries signed an agreement in which France would provide Iran with five nuclear power plants for energy, in return for increased Iranian oil supplies to France

Press Association

Associated Press

Above **30 June: Atlanta, Georgia.** Mrs Martin Luther King, 70, the mother of Martin Luther King, is shot to death while playing the organ in the Ebeneezer Baptist Chapel. While she was playing a man rose from his seat and fired a pistol, killing Mrs King, a man, and wounding another woman. He was overpowered and later stated: 'My name is servant Jacob. I am a Hebrew. I was sent here on a purpose and it is partly accomplished.' He also stated that he killed Mrs King because she was a Christian, and 'all Christians are my enemies'. He was identified as Marcus Chenault, 23. Mrs King's murder comes six years after the murder of her son in Memphis, Tennessee

Press Association

Below **June: Johan Cruyff, 27** (*right*), Holland's football superstar, leaps for the ball — and gets it — in Holland's match against Uruguay. By the end of the first leg of the World Cup, Holland was heavily tipped to become the new World Champion team

Above **27 June: Alert at Heathrow, London**. Police officers check vehicles approaching Heathrow airport as part of a massive security drive on the eve of the visit of the Israeli Prime Minister. A number of foreign VIPs were due to arrive in Britain for the Socialist International Conference, and Special Branch had received information that an attempt might be made on a visiting VIP's life

Left **27 June: Armed troops patrol** Heathrow's number 1 terminal, while a passenger waits for transport held up by the road checks. In spite of delays, passengers' reactions to the security measures were favourable
UPI

Rex Features

Left **28 June: American and Soviet** leaders toast one another after signing an agreement on co-operation on energy research, artificial heart development and housing development. From left to right: Soviet Communist Party leader, Leonid Brezhnev, US President Nixon, Soviet President Nikolai Podgorny, Soviet Premier Alexei Kosygin and Soviet Foreign Minister Andrei Gromyko

Above **13 June: Groups in national dress** parade in the Waldstadium, Munich, to celebrate the opening of the World Cup football series played in West Germany during June and July

Below **18 June: Billy Bremner's face of despair.** Billy Bremner gives vent to his feelings of disgust after he missed an open goal in Scotland's match against Brazil in the 1974 World Cup in Frankfurt. Bremner, Scotland's captain, had only a split-second opportunity – Scotland's only chance that day. The match ended in a no-score draw and Scotland were later put out of the World Cup by Brazil on goal difference

Right **June 1974: The trophy for** which the world's best football teams met to contend during June and July. Produced to replace the Jules Rimet Trophy, the FIFA World Cup was sculpted by **Silvio Gazzaniga** and produced by **Bertoni** of Milan

SPORT

28/29 July 1973: The British Waterskiing Championships held at Biggleswade brought victory in the men's event to **Paul Seaton** and in the women's to **Karen Morse** (*left*). Both went on to represent Britain in the World Championships with Seaton securing 10th place and Morse 13th

Tony Duffy

Tony Duffy

Below **July 1973: A wave of triumph** from **Peter Revson** after winning the 1973 British Grand Prix. Revson was later tragically killed

Don Morley/Sportsworld

Below right **25 August 1973: Crowds appear unperturbed** after a bomb scare at Lords' Cricket Ground, London. All the spectators were asked to leave by the nearest exit and were forbidden to drive their cars out of the ground. The two cricket teams, England and the West Indies, sat in the centre of the pitch surrounded by the police until the grounds had been thoroughly searched. Play was resumed after the all-clear was given

Below left **July 1973: Chris Evert,** runner-up in the All-England, French and Italian Open Championships returns an awkward ball

Colorsport

Press Association

Left **8 September 1973: More action** in a very action-packed year for **Princess Anne** of Great Britain. As she went into the second obstacle on the cross-country course of the European Equestrian Championships at Kiev, USSR, her horse, **Goodwill,** stumbled and down they both came. The Princess received only minor injuries. The obstacle, which was by common consent exceedingly difficult, brought down a number of other competitors

Below left **1 September 1973: Tokyo. Joe King Roman** of Puerto Rico wards off another blow from **George Foreman** as he sits slumped against the ropes having already been knocked down. This punch caused widespread protest, but the fight was ended and Foreman declared winner in one minute 50 seconds of the first round

Bottom left **Roman** (*right*) and **Foreman** (*left*) after the fight

Below right **July 1973: Tom Weiskopf, US,** studies a putt in the British Open at Troon. Weiskopf led in every round and equalled Arnold Palmer's record aggregate with the following number of strokes in each round: 68, 67, 71, 70

Associated Press

Associated Press

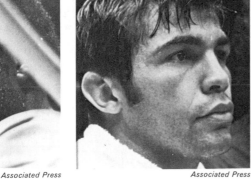

Associated Press

Associated Press

Colorsport

Below **October 1973: Ludmilla Tourischeva, USSR,** goes through her gymnastic routine at the European Championships where she carried away all five gold medals

Right **September 1973: Belgrade Yugoslavia.** Australia's astonishing **Stephen Holland,** 15, chops 14·8 seconds off the record for the 1,500 metres freestyle. He went on to lower his own world record by a further 6 seconds during the first World Swimming Championships

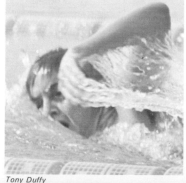

Tony Duffy

Bottom right **October 1973: Poland's** goalie, **Jan Tomaszewski,** saves an attempt at Poland's goal by England in the World Cup qualifier. The 1–1 draw prevented England from qualifying for the final stages of the tournament

Colorsport

**24 January/2 February 1974:
Christchurch, New Zealand.**
Athletes from the Commonwealth
nations come together for the
Commonwealth Games

Right **Commonwealth Games.
Ben Jipcho, Kenya,** leads in the
5,000 metres. He won both this
event and the steeplechase

Below **Commonwealth Games.
Jenny Turrel, Australia,** on her
way to victory in the 400 metres
freestyle for which she gained a
gold medal. She also won two
silvers

Tony Duffy

Below **Commonwealth Games.
Dick Tayler, New Zealand,** flings
up his arms in triumph as he wins
the 10,000 metres track event
cheered on by an enthusiastic home
crowd

Tony Duffy

Colorsport

Tony Duffy

Right **Commonwealth Games.**
Frank Lucas, St Lucia (*right*), wins
a semi-final bout on his way to a
gold medal. His victory was an
ironic one as he had been turned
down by the selectors of the team
for England, his country of resi-
dence, and he boxed instead for St
Lucia, his place of birth

Below **Commonwealth Games.**
Raelene Boyle, Australia (*right*),
wins the women's 100 metres from
Andrea Lynch of England (*left*)

Tony Duffy

Tony Duffy

Left **Commonwealth Games.**
Filbert Bayi, Tanzania, wins the
1,500 metres way ahead of the
opposition. He led from gun to tape
in what was one of the most
sensational performances of the
games

Below **Commonwealth Games.**
Alan Pascoe, England, who won
the 400 metres hurdles, embarras-
singly knocks down not one but
two hurdles as he starts his victory
lap. He abandoned the attempt

Associated Press

Associated Press

E. D. Lacey

2–10 February 1974: Franz Klammer of Austria gets airborne in the Men's Downhill event at St Moritz. In December 1973, he had set up the fastest speed ever recorded in a men's downhill event during a race in Austria

Right **10 February 1974: Gustav Thoeni** rounds a bend in the Giant Slalom event of the World Alpine Ski Championships held in St Moritz. Thoeni won the Giant Slalom and the Special Slalom but failed to gain the combined title as he was not entered for the downhill event

Tony Duffy

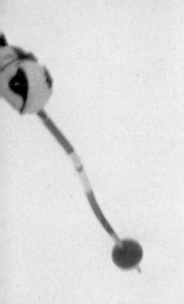

Far left **12 March: Christine Errath** of East Germany competing in the World Ice Skating Championships in Munich, West Germany, where she won the women's title. Dancer-like leaps were a feature of the competitors' repertoires, causing some raised eyebrows among the more old-fashioned spectators

Left **12 March: Errath** cuts a figure of a more conventional kind

Tony Duffy

Tony Duffy

Right **30 March 1974:** **Brian Fletcher** takes the last fence in fine style on Red Rum and gallops on past the post to win the Grand National for the second year running. Red Rum, who was second favourite, carried the top weight of 12 stone and still managed to make mincemeat of his opponents. He was the first horse ever to win three grand nationals within eighteen months. He won the Scottish Grand National in April 1974. His owner said that he was going back into training for the 1975 Grand National. No horse has ever won this punishing race three times

Below **1 April 1974:** April Fool's day is perhaps a suitable date for the first mixed race under Jockey Club rules which was won by last year's Ladies Champion, **Linda Goodwill,** pictured here after her victory on Pee Mai. In fact the ladies gave the men a sound thrashing in the Ladbroke Lads and Lassies Amateur Handicap at Nottingham, taking first, second and third places. The best the men could manage was a fourth by Mr Harry Hodge on March Malona

Popperfoto

Press Association

Left **26 March:** George Foreman smashes a left to **Ken Norton's** head in the second round of their title fight held in Caracas. The blow floored Norton and retained the world heavyweight title for Foreman

Below **8 April 1974:** A jubilant **Hank Aaron** holds up the ball he hit to make the 715th home run of his baseball career. With this run he outstripped **Babe Ruth's** long-standing record to become base-ball's highest scorer

Associated Press   *Associated Press*

Right **May 1974: Crystal Palace, London.** An incident in the European Judo Championships. Judges look on as two competitors fight for a fall

Tony Duffy

Below **June 1974: Ann Moore,** the woman European Showjumping Champion, seen competing at Hickstead in 1973. In 1974 she announced her retirement from showjumping

Tony Duffy

Keystone

Press Association

Associated Press   *Keystone*

Keystone

Far left **June 1974: Rome. Sweden's** tennis wonder-boy, **Bjorn Borg,** holds up the trophy of the Italian Open Championship which he won when he beat **Nastase** of Rumania. With his 18th birthday falling on 6 June, he became the youngest-ever winner of a men's open championship

Top **June 1974: Britain's Virginia Wade** started off her first week at Wimbledon with a string of successes and by the end of June seemed destined to reach the semi-finals, the best effort of her Wimbledon career

Left **27 June 1974: Jim Connors, US,** in his match against Australia's **P. C. Dent.** The match was rained off in what was the wettest Wimbledon since 1952, but when play resumed Connors made no mistake and went forward into the second week of Wimbledon

Above **June 1974: Chris Evert,** US, played so well in the first week of Wimbledon, except for one troublesome match against Australia's **Lesley Hunt,** that by the end of June she looked a certain bet for the women's single finals

Left **June 1974: John Newcombe,** Australia, the number one seed, seemed to be fulfilling his promise as the favourite for the men's singles title by winning all his early matches in easy sets, but, with the tournament about to go into its second week, he had some tough competition ahead of him

Associated Press

Associated Press

Above **22 June 1974: South Africa. Gareth Edwards,** the scrum half of the British Lions touring side breaks away as the scrum collapses during the match in Pretoria between South Africa and the British team. The Lions won the match by a shattering 28–9, the most resounding defeat in the history of South African international rugby

Above right **June 1974: The Lions'** wing forward, **Slattery,** feeds the ball out of a scrum while **Chris Ralston** and **Fran Cotton** (*centre*) shield him during a game against the coloured Capetown side, Proteus. The Lions won, 37–6

Below **20 June 1974: England's David Lloyd** is out, caught, after scoring 46 runs in the first day of the Second Test between England and India at Lord's. England won the match by an innings and 285 runs. In the second innings of the match the Indians were all out for 42, the lowest total in India's international cricket or in any test

at Lord's. In the same match England's score of 629 runs in one innings constituted the highest test score ever made at Lord's. The series continued into July but, having won the first two tests, England were already the undisputed winners

Press Association

Left **4 May 1974:** Kevin Keegan (*second left*) scores Liverpool's first goal in the FA Cup Final against Newcastle United held at Wembley Stadium. Keegan also scored his team's third goal in the 3–0 victory. All the goals came in the second half of the match. Newcastle's goalie, Ian McFaul, hits the ground in a vain attempt to save

June 1974: West Germany. The world's top footballers met to contend for the World Cup. Teams from the Argentine, Australia, Brazil, Bulgaria, Chile, East and West Germany, Haiti, Holland, Italy, Poland, Scotland, Sweden, Uruguay, Yugoslavia and Zaire played a series of matches piling up points until finally Holland and West Germany led the remainder to go through to the final deciding game in July

Left **15 June: Argentina's Ayala** (*right*) gets entangled with Poland's **Adam Musial** as Welsh referee, **Clive Thomas,** looks on. Poland won 3–2

Right **18 June: Yugoslavia's Branko Oblak** puts the ball home as Zaire's goalie, **Muamba Kazadi,** beats the ground with fury

Right **22 June: West and East Germany meet. Gerd Müller** (West Germany, white shirt) is stopped by **Konrad Weise** of East Germany. East Germany won the match, but West Germany went on to the final

Right **15 June: Johan Cruyff,** Holland's number 14, clears the ball from Julio Montero, Uruguay's number 5, during Holland's 2—0 victory over Uruguay at Hanover during the World Cup series

Below **22 June: A strong shot** by Scotland's **Bremner** and a good save by Yugoslavia's goalie, **Enver Maric,** as the two teams met at Frankfurt. They tied 1—1, but Scotland, who needed a win to remain in the tournament, were knocked out

Press Association

Associated Press

INDEX

A

Aaron, Hank 211
Aberfan (Wales) 125
Acali love raft 35
Addis Ababa (Ethiopia) 144
Adventure 154
Afghanistan 15
Agnew, Vice-President Spiro T. 30, 57
Aikman, Megan 136
Ain Helweh (Lebanon) 181
Aircrashes
    France 9, 139–40
    Samoa 119
Al Ahram 127
Al Badshhi Mosque, Lahore (Pakistan) 136
Alexandra, Princess 167, 197
Algeria 44
Alibey Pass, battle of (Iraq) 157
Allende, President Salvador 36, 49
American Indian movement 116, 122
Amin, Ali 127
Amin, General Idi 147
Andrew, Prince 73
Androutsopoulos, Adamantios 87
Anne, Princess 73, 129, 141, 203
Arab-Israeli war (1973) 65–7, 77, 80, 117
    peace conference, Geneva 117, 173
Argentina football team 215
Armstrong-Jones, Lady Sarah 73
Army School of Catering (GB) 73
Arube, Brigadier Charles 147
ASLEF, industrial action by 102, 110, 133 f
Associated Newspapers Ltd 162
Associated Society of Locomotive Engineers and Firemen, see *ASLEF*
Association of Tennis Professionals 21
Athens (Greece) 79
Athens airport massacre 31
Athletics 205 ff
Atlanta, Georgia 71, 198
Australia 61, 112
Austria 55
Ayala, Ruben 215

B

Badawi, Major-General 96
Bahamas 15, 34
Baker, Senator Howard H. 13
Ball, Ian 141
Bandaranaike, Mrs Sirimavo 34
Bangkok (Thailand) 58
Bangkok airport, picketing of 113
Bangladesh 34, 135
Bank robberies
    Champigny-sur-Marne (France) 184
    Hamburg (W Germany) 163
    San Francisco (US) 160
    Stockholm (Sweden) 37
Banks, Dennis 122
Banks, Gordon 39
Bar Lev line 66
Barbados 34
Barber, Anthony 107
Barr, Glen 191
Barrow, Errol 34
Barzani, General Mullah Mustafa 157
Baseball 211
Bates, Herbert Ernest 115
Bayi, Filbert 207
Bean, Alan 24, 55
Beaton, Inspector James Wallace 141
Beit, Lady 195
Beit, Sir Alfred 189, 195
Belfast (N Ireland) 53, 148
Belgrade (Yugoslavia) 44, 204
Ben Gurion, David 95
Benghazi airfield (Libya) 17
Berkeley, California 122
Berry, Angie 184
Bertoni 200
Best, George 138
Bhutan 187
Bhutto, Ali 135
Biggleswade (GB) 201
Biggs, Ronald 131
Bird, Peter 141
Black hole' stars 85
Black Teachers Caucus (US) 122
Blanco, Admiral Carrero 104
Bloom, Metropolitan Anthony 160
Böll, Heinrich 121
Borg, Bjorn 213
Bosphorus Bridge 82
Botswana 34
Le Bourget airport, Paris 45
Boxing 203, 206, 211
Boyle, Raelene 206
Brandt, Willy 176
Brazil 131
Brazil football team 200, 215
Bremner, Billy 200, 216
Brescia (Italy) 178
Brezhnev, Leonid 199
Brisbane (Australia) 112
British Broadcasting Corporation (BBC), Belfast 188

British Commonwealth 15
British Open Golf Championships (1973) 203
British Rail 110
British Waterskiing Championships (1973) 200
Buendia, Father Miguel 22
Bulgaria football team 215
Burton, Richard 11, 168
Buskers Festival 136
Butler, James 184
Butterfield, Alexander P. 13

Caetano, Dr Marcello 22, 151, 164, 179
Cairo (Egypt) 23, 193
Calcutta (India) 172
Caldas da Rainta (Portugal) 151
Callender, Alexander 141
Camara, Vice-President Andrew 34
Cambridge University boat crew 155
Canada 34
Canary Isles 35
Canterbury Cathedral 137
Cap de la Hague 71
Cape Canaveral (US) 85
Caprolactam 187
Car racing 13, 59, 184, 202
Caracas (Venezuela) 211
Caribbean, The 35
Carl XVI Gustaf, King of Sweden 56
Carr, Gerald P. 85
Carrington, Lord 195
de Carvalho, Major 188
Casals, Pablo 69
Cassidy, David 182
de Castro, Raimunda 131
Central Dumbartonshire (Scotland) 134
Champigny-sur-Marne (France) 184
Channel Tunnel 41
Channon, Mike 63
Chantilly (France) 191
Chapman, Roger 56
Charles, Prince of Wales 15, 73, 182, 190
Charles de Gaulle airport, Paris 147
Chasewater Lake, Staffordshire 162
Chelsea Registry Office, London 15
Chenault, Marcus 198
Chevening Place, Kent 182
Chichester, Sir Francis 149
Chile 36, 49, 101
Chile football team 215
China 15, 43, 185
Chinese Exhibition, London 43
Chirac, Jacques 198
Chogyal of Sikkim 187
Cholera 26
Chona, Vice-President Mainza 34
Chou En-lai 43
Christchurcn (New Zealand) 205
Christophides, John 34
Cincinnati, Ohio 156
Civil Rights Lists party (Israel) 127
Clough, Brian 63
'Cod war' 69
Coggan, Dr Donald 178
Colas, Alain 149
Colson, Charles 142
Common Market – see European Economic Community

Commonwealth Conference (1973) 34
Commonwealth Games (1974) 205–7
Concorde 123
Congressional Committee on Internal Revenue (US) 156
Connors, Jim 213
Conservative Party (GB) 133 f, 138, 195
Copernicus satellite 85
Corll, Dean 30
Cosgrave, Liam 103
Cotton, Fran 214
Council for Civil Liberties (GB) 163
Council of Ireland 103
Country Matters 215
Coups d'etat
    Afghanistan 15
    Chile 49, 101
    Greece 79
    Portugal 164
    Uganda (attempted) 147
Cox, Archibald 13, 62
Cozumel (Mexico) 35
Craig, William 191
Cricket 202, 214
Crown Court, Winchester 75
Cruyff, Johan 199, 216
Crystal Palace, London 212
Cup Final, Wembley 215
Currie, Tony 63
Cyprus 19, 34, 77, 112

Darling Buds of May, The 115
Davey, Timothy 182
Davis, Rusty 148
Dayan, Moshe 127, 132, 160
Dean, John 13, 87
Deep Throat 191
Delhi station (India) 172
Delmas, Jacques Chaban 177
Democratic Labour candidate (GB) 133 f
Dent, P.C. 213
Derby, The (1974) 197
Derby County Football Club 63
Devlin, Bernadette 114
DGS (Portuguese state police) 164
Dharmasak, Professor Sanya 58
Diab, Mohamed 44
Dickens and Jones (department store), London 40
Divorce laws (Italy) 178
Djebel Zebair 126
Dlamini, Prince 34
Dodd, Warrant-Officer David 73
Doig, David 168
Dona Marika 30
Donoughmore, Lady 189
Donoughmore, Lord 189
Douglas-Home, Sir Alec 89
Downpatrick counting centre (N Ireland) 10
Druk Gyalpo, the Dragon King 187
Dubai airfield (Persian Gulf) 17
Dublin (Republic of Ireland) 175
Duc Hue Ranger Base (S Vietnam) 159
Dugdale, Dr Rose 195
Duke of York's barracks, London 53

Dungannon (N Ireland) 130
Dunlop, John 114
Durban (S Africa) 115
Düsseldorf (W Germany) 80

East African Safari Rally (1974) 168
East Germany football team 215
Ebeneezer Baptist Chapel, Atlanta 198
Edinburgh, Duke of 34, 61, 73, 129, 138, 190, 197
Edward, Prince 73
Edwards, Gareth 214
Egypt
    Arab-Israeli war (1973) 65–7, 77
    Army command changes 96
    Heykal removed 127
    Libya, political merger with 23, 36
    Navy 154
    Nixon visit 192
    Third Army 66 f, 77, 96
Ehrlichman, John 142
Eilat, Gulf of 118
Eire – see Ireland, Republic of
Ekland, Britt 183
Election – see General Election (GB)
Electrical engineers (GB), industrial action by 107, 124, 133
Elizabeth, Queen 34, 39, 61, 73, 129, 138, 190 f, 197
Elizabeth, Queen, Queen Mother 73, 197
Ellsberg, Dr Daniel 142
Empire Pool, Wembley 46
Ender, Cornelia 21
England cricket team 202, 214
England football team 63, 184, 204
EOKA underground movement (Cyprus) 19
Ermonville, Forest of (France) 139
Errath, Christine 209
Ervin, Senator Sam 13
Essex University (GB) 148
ETA (Basque Separatist group) 104
Ethiopia 144
Etiang, Paul 34
European Economic Community (EEC) 99, 134, 176
European Equestrian Championships (1973) 203
European Gymnastics Championships (1973) 204
European Judo Championships (1974) 212
European Security Conference 89
Euston Station, London 53
Evert, Chris 21, 202, 213

Fair Stood the Wind for France 115
Farah, Empress 198

Farmers' demonstration, Paris 142
Farrow, Mia 150
Faulkner, Brian 10, 103, 114, 174
Feather, Victor 112
Federal Bureau of Investigation (FBI) 160
Feeney, Hugh 189
Feisal, King of Saudi Arabia 136, 193
Fell, Father Patrick 75
Femme Assise 93
Ferando, Father Enrique 22
FIFA World Cup 200
Fiji 34
Finnen, Mrs Francis 170
First Regiment, Royal Horse Artillery 148
Fitzgerald, Scott 147
Fletcher, Brian 210
Flixborough (GB) 187
Floods
    Australia 112
    Pakistan 37
    Spain 70
Football 39, 63, 184, 199, 204, 215
Ford, Gerald 57, 104
Foreman, George 203, 211
Formula I John Player Special Lotus 13
Fouka (Egypt) 23
France
    aircrashes 9, 139–40
    anti-racism demonstration 44
    Channel Tunnel 41
    Charles de Gaulle airport inaugurated 147
    elections 177
    farmers' demonstration 142
    Lip watch factory, workers take over 27
    Messmer, resignation and re-instatement of 126
    nuclear tests 14, 187
    Pompidou, death of 153
    Saudi Arabian Embassy, Paris, terrorist attack 45
    Servan-Schreiber dismissed 187
    Shah of Iran visit 198
Franco, General Francisco 104
Frankfurt (W Germany) 200, 216
Frelimo liberation movement 188
Friends of the Earth environmentalist pressure group 195
Frogmore (GB) 190
Funfrock, Mme Hugette 39

Gaddafi, President Moamar 23, 36, 136
Gairy, Eric 131
Gamassy, Major-General 96
Gambia, The 34
Garriott, Owen 24, 55
Gatch, Thomas 123
Gately, Kevin 194 f
Gaughan, Michael 188
Gazzaniga, Silvio 200
Geller, Uri 97
General Election (GB) 133–5, 138, 195

Geneva peace conference on the Arab-Israeli war 117, 173
Germany, East 27, 176
Germany, West 121, 163, 176, 200, 215
Getty, Paul 11, 95
Getty junior, Paul 11, 95, 151
Ghana 34
Ghizikis, Lieutenant-General Phaedon 87
Giacometti 197
Giant Slalom event, World Alpine Ski Championships (1974) 208
Gibson, Edward G. 85
Giscard d'Estaing, Mme 198
Giscard d'Estaing, President Valéry 126, 176 f, 187, 198
Glide Memorial Methodist Church (US) 122
Gloucester, Duke of 190
Goat's Head Soup 46
Golan Heights (Israel) 65 ff, 166, 173
Golden, Yvonne 122
Golf 203·
Goodwill 203
Goodwill, Linda 210
Gormley, Joe 108, 124
Goroka Park (Papua New Guinea) 129
Government Printing Office, Washington 170
Gowon, General Y. 34
Grable, Betty 19
Grand Central Hotel, Belfast 148
Grand National (1974) 210
Grand National (1974), Scottish 210
Grand Prix
    Belgian Formula (1973) 59
    British (1973) 202
    French (1973) 13
    Monte Carlo (1974) 184
Great Britain (GB) 22, 131, 154, 163, 185
    Channel Tunnel 41
    'Cod war' 69
    death of Duke of Gloucester 190
    General Election 133–5, 138, 195
    Healey budget 140
    industrial action by ASLEF 102, 110, 133 f; electrical workers 107, 124, 133
    'land deals' affair 162
    Latimer National Defence College bombed 130
    mineworkers' work-to-rule 102, 106 f; strike 107 ff, 124–5, 133
    nurses' pay claims 173
    Nypro factory explosion, Flixborough 187
    (See also London)
Great Gatsby, The 147
Greece 87
    amnesty for political offenders 40
    Athens airport massacre 31
    coup 79
    Grivas, death of 112
    referendum 14
    Serafeim, Mgr, elected 108
Grenada 131
Gromyko, Andrei 89, 199
Grounds, Captain Eric 73
Grivas, General George 19, 112
Gueffen, Manachen 15
Guillaume, Gunther 176
Guinness Book of Records 171

Gulag Archipelago, The 121
Guru Maharaj Ji, The 179
Gustaf VI Adolf, King of Sweden 56
Guyana 34
Gymnastics 204

Haig, General Alexander 170
Haile Selassie, Emperor of Ethiopia 144
Haiti football team 215
el Hakkaoui, Abelkhir 119
Hale Observatories, California 93
Halley, George 93
Hamburg (W Germany) 163
Hanover (W Germany) 216
Harrisburg Airport, Pennsylvania 123
Harrods (department store), London 40
Hastings, Father Adrian 22
Hawkins, Jack 15
Healey, Denis 140
Hearst, Patricia 122, 160
Hearst, Randolph 122
Heath, Edward 34, 69, 133, 138, 185, 192
Heathrow Airport, London 111, 139, 199
Hencken, John 44
Henley, Wayne 30
Herron, Tommy 53
Heykal, Muhammad Hassanein 127
Hibernian Bank, San Francisco 160
Hickstead (GB) 19, 212
Highclere 191
Highway 4, Phnom Penh (Khmer Republic) 32
Hijackings 17, 88
Hills, PC Michael 141
Hine, PC Malcolm 75
Hodge, Harry 210
Hoffman, Martin 215
Holland 80, 99
Holland, Stephen 204
Holland football team 199, 215 f
Honecker, Erich 27
Hong Kong 185
Horse racing 191, 197, 210
House Judiciary Committee (US) 170
Houses of Parliament (GB) 196
Hughes, Howard 170
Hunt, Lesley 213
Hussein, King of Jordan 48

Ice skating 209
Iceland 69
Immortal Tales 167
Imperial Prince 197
Independent Labour candidate 133 f, 138

India 34, 135, 172, 187
India cricket team 214
Indo-China — See *Khmer Republic and Vietnam*
Indonesia 113
Industrial Relations Act (GB) 133
Institute of Scientific Research, Stanforth University, California 97
International Control Commission (Vietnam) 159
International Council of Music, 25th Anniversary of 105
International Telephone and Telegraph Corporation (ITT) 110
International Whaling Commission 195
Iran 198
Iraq 65f, 157
Ireland, Republic of 175, 195
Irish Republican Army (IRA) Provisionals 40, 53, 70, 75, 103, 130, 163, 188f, 196
Isle of Man 38
Israel 48, 192f
    Arab-Israeli war (1973) 65–7, 77, 117
    Ben Gurion, death of 95
    Maalot school massacre 180f
    Meir resigns 160; retires 185
    minority government formed 127
    Mount Hermon, fight for 166
    Nixon visit 192
    peace conference, Geneva 117, 173
    withdrawal of forces 132
Israeli basketball team 40
Italian Open Tennis Championship (1974) 213
Italy
    bomb explosion, Brescia 178
    cholera outbreak 26
    divorce laws 178
    Getty kidnapping 11, 95, 151
    Rome Airport terrorist attack 101
    Rumour appointed 10
Italy football team 215

Jackson, Maynard 71
Jagger, Mick 46
Jakarta (Indonesia) 113
Jamaica 34
Japan 58, 88, 99, 113, 143, 195
Japan Air Lines 17
Japanese Embassy, Kuwait 135
Japanese Red Army 135
Jeddah (Saudi Arabia) 193
Jenkins, Roy 189
Jerusalem (Israel) 193
Jews, Soviet 55
Jey Kehmpo 187
Jigme Singh Wangchuk, King of Bhutan 187
Jipcho, Ben 205
Jobert, Michel 126
Johannesson, Olafur 69
Johnson, Marolyn Lois 179
Jonathan, Chief Leabua 34

Jones, Janie 162
Jones, Tom 138
Jordan 65f, 192
Juan Carlos, Prince 104
Judo 212
Jules Rimet Trophy 200
Jupiter 90

Kaye, Danny 82
Kazadi, Muamba 215
Keegan, Kevin 215
Kelly, Gerald 189
Kempff, Wilhelm 105
Kennedy, Senator Edward 143, 161
Kennedy junior, Edward 143
Kennedy, Joseph 39
Kent, Duke of 190
Kenya 34
Khama, Sir Seretse 34
Khan, General Daud 15
Khanpur (Pakistan) 37
Khir Johari 34
Khmer Republic 20, 32f, 51, 109, 128
Khmer Rouge insurgents 109
Khyber Pass (Afghanistan) 15
Kien Duc (Vietnam) 92
Kiev (USSR) 203
Kilometre 101, talks at 77, 117
King, Billie Jean 21, 50, 202
King, Derek 141
King, Martin Luther 198
King, Mrs Martin Luther 198
King Street, Belfast 53
King's Cross Station, London 53
Kirk, Norman 34
Kirkuk region (Iraq) 157
Kirov Ballet (USSR) 192
Kissinger, Dr Henry 61, 132, 152, 159, 173, 185
Kittikachorn, Marshal Thanom 58
Klammer, Franz 208
Kodes, Jan 21
Kohoutek (comet) 93
Kohoutek, Lubos 93
Kompong Cham (Khmer Republic) 51
Kosygin, Alexei 199
Kumamoto (Japan) 88
Kuneitra (Israel) 67
Kurdish revolt (Iraq) 157
Kuwait 101, 135

Labour Alignment Party (Israel) 127, 185
Labour Party (GB) 133f, 138
Lacheteau, Xavier 184
Ladbroke Lads and Lassies Amateur Handicap, Nottingham 210

Lahore (Pakistan) 135
'Land deals' affair (GB) 162
Langenbroich (W Germany) 121
Larnaca Road police station, Nicosia 19
Larne, Co Antrim (N Ireland) 174
Lassen, Brigadier N.Y. Ashley 34
Latimer National Defence College (GB) 130
Lawn tennis — see *Tennis*
Le Duc Tho 61, 159
Lebanon 48, 181
Lee Kuan Yew 34
Lennon, Kenneth 163
Lesotho 34
Liberal Party (GB) 133ff, 138, 195
'Liberation' group (GB) 194
Liberty's (department store), London 40
Libya 17, 23, 36, 99
Libyan Revolutionary Command Council 23
Likud and Tora Religious Front (Israel) 127
Lindsway Bay, Pembrokeshire 30
Lions, British rugby team 214
Lip watch factory (France) 27
Lisbon (Portugal) 151, 169
Liverpool Football Club 215
Liverpool Street Station, London 102
Lloyd, David 214
Loew's Theatre, New York 147
Lon Nol, President 20
London
    bomb incidents 40, 53, 75, 103, 196, 202
    IRA march 188
    Red Lion Square riot 194f
London Press Association 196
London Symphony Orchestra 192
London Tourist Board 136
London Zoo 185
Londonderry (N Ireland) 130
Long Kesh internment camp (N Ireland) 28
Lords' Cricket Ground, London 202, 214
Lorry-drivers' strike (Chile) 36
Los Angeles, California 171
Lousma, Jack 24, 55
Lovelace, Linda 191
Lucas, Frank 206
Luga Airport (Malta) 88
Lugbara tribe (Uganda) 147
Lusaka (Zambia) 188
Luton, Bedfordshire 163
Lynch, Andrea 206

Maalot school massacre (Israel) 180f
McConnell, Brian 141
McFarland, Roy 63
McFaul, Ian 215
McGahey, Mick 107f
Machel, President Samora 188
McMahon, Paddy 19
Madeley, Paul 63
Madrid (Spain) 104
Maginnes, Nancy Sharon 152

Makarios, President 112, 179
Malawi 34
Malaysia 34
Malinson, Roger 56
Mallon, Keven
Maloney, Sir Joseph 75
Malta 34, 88
Man With the Golden Gun, The 183
Manley, Michael 34
Manureva 149
Mao Tse-tung 43, 179
Mara, Ratu Sir Kamisese 34
March Malona 210
'Marchers to Egypt' 23
Margaret 71
Maric, Enver 216
Marshall and Snelgrove (department
    store), London 40
Maryland (US) 30, 57
Mata'afa, Fiame 34
Mauritius 34
Maystone, Carol 141
Means, Russell 116
Mecca organisation (GB) 138
Meir, Mrs Golda 127, 160, 185
Mekong Delta (S Vietnam) 92, 159
Men's Downhill event, St Moritz
    208
Men's European Show Jumping
    Championship (1973), Hick-
    stead (GB) 19
Menuhin, Yehudi 105
Mercer, Joe 184
Merrick, David 147
Mersa Matruh (Egypt) 23
Messmer, Pierre 126, 147
Methodist Hospital, Indianapolis
    188
Metreveli, Alexander 21
Middle East 89
    Nixon visit 192-3
    (See also *Arab-Israeli war* and
        respective countries)
Midway 58
Milhench, Kathleen 162
Milhench, Ronald 162
Miller, Ellen 170
Mills, Wilbur 156
Mineworkers (GB)
    work-to-rule 102, 106f
    strike 107ff, 124-5, 133
Mintoff, Dom 34
Mitchell, John 13
Mitterand, François 177
Moi, Vice-President Daniel Arap 34
Moked Party (Israel) 127
Monaghan (Republic of Ireland)
    175
Mongoose Squad (Grenada) 131
Montero, Julio 216
Moore, Ann 212
Moore, Roger 183
Moreno, Tomas 183
Morocco 65
Morris, James 136
Morse, Karen 201
Moscow Student Games 40
Mount Hermon 66, 117, 166
Mount Herzl military cemetery
    (Israel) 132
Mountjoy Jail (Eire) 70
Mozambique 22, 188
Msonthi, J. B. 34
Muhammad Reza Pahlevi, Shah of
    Iran 198
Müller, Gerd 215
Munich (W Germany) 209
Murcia (Spain) 70
Murray, Len 107, 112
Mururoa Atoll 14
Musial, Adam 215

Nabarro, Sir Gerald 84
Naples (Italy) 26
Nassau (Bahamas) 15
Nasseem, Ather 119
Nastase, Ilie 213
National Coal Board (NCB) 107
National Front (GB) 194
National Gallery, Dublin 195
National Religions Party (Israel) 127
National Union of Mineworkers
    (NUM) 107ff, 124
Nationalisation (Chile) 36
Nelson, Peter 197
New Hebrides 129
New Orleans (US) 25
New Orleans 55
New Zealand 14, 34, 129, 205
Newcastle United Football Club 215
Newcombe, John 213
Newtonabbey (N Ireland) 120
Nicosia (Cyprus) 19
Nigeria 34
Nixon, President Richard 13, 25, 62,
    87, 142, 156, 170, 192-3, 199
Nobel Peace Prize (1973) 61
Nonoalco 197
Northern Ireland 35, 102
    bomb explosions 53, 130, 148
    election 10
    Faulkner resigns from Unionist
        Party 114; from N Ireland
        executive 174
    Newtonabbey murders 120
    People's Democracy march 28
    Sunningdale agreement 103,
        191
    Ulster Protestants' strike 174
Norton, Ken 211
Notre Dame cathedral, Paris 153
Nottingham (GB) 210
Nuclear tests 14, 172, 187
Nurses' pay claims (GB) 173
Nyerere, Julius 34
Nypro factory, Flixborough (GB)
    187

Oblak, Branko 215
O'Brien, Michael 167
October war — See *Arab-Israeli war*
Odonga, Michael 147
O'Hagan, Joe 70
Oil crisis 80, 99, 102, 107, 124, 133
Okamoto, Kozo 17
Olsson, Jan Erik 37
Olympics of the Absurd (US) 171
Onado, Lieutenant Hiroo 143
Organisation of African Unity 147
Orly Airport, Paris 9
Orvilliers (France) 153
Otago 14
Ottawa (Canada) 34

Oxford and Cambridge boat race
    155
Oxford University boat crew 155

Paisley, Rev Ian 191
Pakistan 37, 135, 187
Palmer, Arnold 203
Panaghoulis, Alexander 40
Panov, Galina 192
Panov, Valery 192
Papadopulous, President 14, 79
Papua New Guinea 129
Parkhurst Prison (Isle of Wight) 188
Pascoe, Alan 207
Pay Board (GB) 107
Pee Mai 210
Peking (China) 43, 179
Pembrokeshire (Wales) 30
Pentonville Prison, London 103
Penwood Forgemill 19
People's Democracy protest march
    (N Ireland) 28
Peters, Martin 63, 184
Peterson, Ronnie 13, 184
PFLP — See *Popular Front for the
    Liberation of Palestine*
Philip, Prince — See *Edinburgh,
    Duke of*
Philippines, The 143
Phillips, Captain Mark 73, 129, 141
Phillips, Neil 197
Phillips, Peter 73
Phillips, Mrs Peter 73
Phnom Penh (Khmer Republic) 20,
    32f, 51, 109, 128
Phoenix Park, Dublin 189
Picasso, Pablo 93, 167
Picasso, Paloma 167
Pindling, Lynden O. 15, 34
Pioneer 10 90
Piromalli, Girolamo 151
Pisces III 56
Podgorny, Nikolei 199
Pogue, William P. 85
Poland football team 63, 204, 215
Pompidou, President Georges 43,
    126, 153
Popular Front for the Liberation of
    Palestine (PFLP) 135
Portugal
    attempted coup, March, 1974
        151
    successful coup, April, 1974
        164, 169
    Mozambique, conference on
        188
    Spinola elected President 179
    Wiriyamu, alleged massacre in
        22
Pottinger, William 135
Poulson, John 135
Powell, Enoch 134
Pretoria (S Africa) 214
Prevatt, Francis 34
Previn, André 150, 192
Previn, Fletcher Farrow 150
Price, Dolours 75, 189
Price, Marion 75, 189
Prix de Diane 191
Proteus rugby team 214
Provisional IRA — See *Irish Repub-
    lican Army (IRA) Provisionals*

QE 2 93, 155
Queensland (Australia) 112

Rabin, Yitzhak 185
Racing – See Car racing and Horse racing
Rafael, Gideon 111
Rahman, Sheikh Mujibur 34, 135
Rail strike (India) 172
Railwayworkers' dispute (GB) –See ASLEF
Ralston, Chris 214
Ramgoolam, Sir 34
Ramphal, S. 34
Ramsay, Sir Alf 184
Ramsey, Dr Michael 137, 178
Ravi, River (Pakistan) 37
Rawlinson, Attorney General Sir Peter 75
Red Lion Square riot, London 194f
Red Rum 210
'Red spot' (Jupiter) 90
Reed, Oliver 191
Reid, Jimmy 134
Revson, Peter 138, 202
Richard, Prince of Gloucester 190
Richardson, Elliot 62
Rigg, Diana 15
Riggs, Bobby 50
Rio de Janeiro (Brazil) 131
Riverbank House, London 195
Rolling Stones 46
Roman, Joe King 203
Rome (Italy) 11, 213
Rome Airport terrorist attack 101
Rostropovich, Mstislav 105
Royal Academy, London
    Chinese Exhibition 43
    Summer Exhibition 184
Royal Ascot 191, 197
Royal Avenue, Belfast 148
Royal Navy (GB) 154
Rucklehaus, William 62
Rugby 214
Rumour, Signor Mariano 10
Russborough House, Co Wicklow 195
Russell, Ken 191
Ruth, Babe 211

Sabah, Sheikh of Kuwait 136
Sadat, President Anwar 23, 36, 96, 127, 193
Saigon (S Vietnam) 92

St George's Chapel, Windsor 190
St Lucia 206
St Mary's Roman Catholic Church, Belfast 148
St Moritz (Switzerland) 208
Salle Playel, Paris 105
Samaritaine (shop) 39
Samoa 119
Santa Maria basilica, Florence 178
Santiago (Chile) 49
Sasa (Syria) 66
Saturn 1B rocket 85
Saudi Arabia 65f, 192f
Saudi Arabian Embassy, Paris 45
Sayula II 154
Schmidt, Helmut 176
Schoenau Castle transit camp (Austria) 35
Scotland football team 200, 215f
Scottish Nationalist Party 133f, 138
Sea Venture 155
Seaton, Paul 201
Second Islamic Summit, Lahore 135f
Selfridges (department store), London 40
Senate Watergate Committee (US) 13, 170
Serafeim, Mgr 108
Servan-Schreiber, Jean-Jacques 187
Sharaqpur (Pakistan) 37
Shevlin, Myles 195
Showjumping 19, 212
Sierra Leone 34
Sihanoukist rebels 20, 51
Silasvuo, General Ensio 173
Sinai desert (Israel) 65f
Singapore 34
Singh, Joginder 168
Singh, Swaran 34
Sioux indians 116
Skiing 208
Skylab missions 24, 55, 85
    Skylab 1 24
    Skylab 2 24, 55
    Skylab 3 85
Slattery, J. Fergus 214
Sloman, Dr Albert 148
Snow Knight 197
Soares, Mario 188
Social Democratic and Labour Party (GB) 133
Socialist International conference (1974) 199
Socialist Unity Party (E Germany) 27
Solzhenitsyn, Alexander 105, 121, 150, 160
Solzhenitsyn, Natalya 150
Sotheby's, London 93
South Africa 115
South Africa rugby team 214
South Dakota (US) 116
South Parade Pier, Southsea 191
Southsea (GB) 191
Spain 70, 104
Special Branch (GB) 163, 199
Special Slalom event, World Alpine Ski Championships (1974), St Moritz 208
Spinola, General Antonio S. R. de 164, 179
Sri Lanka 34
Stanhope, Lord 182
Star of Shaddia 126
State of Emergency (GB) 107
Stevens, Dr Siaka 34
Stewart, Jackie 59
Stockholm (Sweden) 37
Stoke City Football Club 39
Stoph, Willy 27

'Streaking' (GB) 167
Strikes
    ASLEF (GB) 110
    Ethiopia 144
    Grenada 131
    India 172
    mineworkers (GB) 107ff, 124–5, 133
    textile workers (S Africa) 115
    Ulster Protestants 174
Sucko, Bob 188
Suez (Egypt) 66f, 77
Suez Canal 66, 117, 132, 154
    East Bank 66, 117, 132
    West Bank 65ff, 117, 132
Summerlands holiday complex (Isle of Man) 38
Sunningdale agreement on the future of Ireland 103, 114, 174, 191
Swaziland 34
Sweden 37, 56
Sweden football team 215
Swimming 21, 44, 204f
Sydney Opera House (Australia) 61
Symbionese Liberation Army (US) 122, 160
Syria 48
    Arab-Israeli war (1973) 65ff
    Mount Hermon, fight for 166
    Nixon visit 192
    peace conference, Geneva 117, 173
    prisoners, exchange of 132

Taiyo department store, Kumamoto (Japan) 88
Tanaka, Kakuei 113
Tanzania 34
Taschichhodzong fortress, Thimpu (Bhutan) 187
Taylor, Dick 205
Taylor, Elizabeth 11, 168
Taylor, Peter 63
Tebura 149
Tennis 21, 50, 202, 213
Terrorism
    Athens Airport massacre 31
    hijackings 17, 88
    Japanese Embassy, Kuwait 135
    Maalot school massacre (Israel) 180
    Rome Airport 101
    Saudi Arabian Embassy, Paris 45
    Soviet Jews kidnapping, (Austria) 55
Textile workers' strike, Durban 115
Thailand 32, 58, 113, 183
Thames Embankment, London 195
Thimpu (Bhutan) 187
Thoeni, Gustav 208
Thomas, Cledwyn 125
Thomas, Clive 215
Thompson, Alison 119
Thorpe, Jeremy 135, 138
Times, The 22
Tokyo (Japan) 99, 203
Tomaszewski, Jan 63, 204
Tommy 191
Tonga 34

Tourischeva, Ludmilla 204
Toyota car offices, Jakarta 113
Trade Union Congress (TUC) 107,
    112
Trinidad and Tobago 34
Trio of the Archduke, The 105
Triple Echo, The 115
Troon (GB) 203
Trudeau, Pierre 34
Tu'Ipelehake, Prince 34
Turkey 182
Turrel, Jenny 205
Twickenham rugby ground 167
Two Sisters, The 115
Twomey, Seamus 70

Uganda 34, 147
Ulbricht, Walter 27
Ulster — See *Northern Ireland*
Ulster protestants 103, 174
Ulster Unionist Party — See *United
    Ulster Unionist Party*
**Union of Soviet Socialist
    Republic (USSR)** 105, 121,
    160, 192, 195
    Douglas-Hume visit 89
    Kennedy visit 161
    Moscow Student Games 40
    USA, agreement with 199
United Nations (UN) 66, 77, 132
United States of America (US)
    Agnew denouces bribery
        charges 30; resigns 57
    Ford elected Vice-President 57
    Hearst kidnapping 122, 160
    indictment of Ehrlichman and
        Colson 142
    Indo-China 20, 32, 51
    Navy 154
    Nixon's income tax 156;
        Middle East visit 192–3
    Skylab missions 24, 55, 85
    USSR, agreement with 199
    Watergate 13, 25, 62, 87, 142,
        170
    Wounded knee, siege of 116
United Ulster Unionist Party 10,
    114, 133, 138
Uruguay football team 199, 215f

Vakis, Christos 19
Versailles Palace (France) 198
Vienna (Austria) 55, 192
Vietnam, North 92, 159
Vietnam, South 20, 92, 159
Vietnam ceasefire agreement 61,
    159

Wade, Virginia 213
Waldstadium, Munich 200
Wales (GB) 106
Wallace, Marjorie 83, 138, 188
Watergate affair (US) 13, 25, 62,
    87, 142, 170
Waterskiing 201
Weed, Stephen 122
Weise, Konrad 215
Weiskopf, Tom 203
Welsh Nationalist Party 133f, 138
West, Harry 191
West Germany football team 215
West Indies cricket team 202
Western Samoa 34
Westminster Hall, London 196
Whales 195
Whitbread round-the-world race
    (1974) 154
White City Stadium, London 182
White House demonstration (US)
    62
Whitelaw, William 102, 108, 195
Whitlam, Gough 34, 61
Wilkie, David 44
Williams, Rev Cecil 122
Williams, Marcia 182
Wilson, Harold 134, 138, 162, 182,
    195
Wilson, Richard 116
**Wimbledon Lawn Tennis
    Championships**
    1973 21, 202
    1974 213
Windsor Castle 190
Windsor Park 138
Wiriyamu village (Mozambique) 22
Woods, Rose Mary 87
World Alpine Ski Championships
    (1974), St Moritz 208
World contest, Miss 83, 138, 188
World Cup football series 63, 199f,
    204, 215f
World Ice Skating Championships
    (1974) 209
World Swimming Championships
    (1973) 204
World Waterskiing Championships
    (1973) 201
Worthington, Frank 184
Wounded Knee, siege of 116

Yokosuka (Japan) 58
Yom Kippur war — See *Arab-Israeli
    war*
Yugoslavia football team 215f

Zahir Shah, King of Afghanistan 15
Zaire football team 215
Zambia 34, 188
Ziegler, Ron 25
Zurich (Switzerland) 121